Preparing international proposals

Robert E. Bartlett

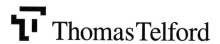
Thomas Telford

Published by Thomas Telford Publishing, Thomas Telford Services Ltd, 1 Heron Quay, London E14 4JD

First published 1997

Distributors for Thomas Telford books are
USA: American Society of Civil Engineers, Publications Sales Department, 345 East 47th Street, New York, NY 10017 – 2398
Japan: Maruzen Co. Ltd, Book Department, 3 – 10 Nihonbashi 2-chome, Chuoku, Tokyo 103
Australia: DA Books and Journals, 648 Whitehorse Road, Mitcham 3132, Victoria

A catalogue record for this book is available from the British Library

ISBN: 0 7277 2582 3

Throughout this book the personal pronoun 'he', 'his', etc. are used when referring to 'the consultant', 'the client', etc. for reasons of readability. Clearly it is quite possible these hypothetical characters may be female in 'real-life' situations, so readers should consider these pronouns to be grammatically neuter in gender, rather than masculine, in all cases.

Typeset in Great Britain by WestKey Limited, Falmouth, Cornwall
Printed in Great Britain by Redwood Books, Trowbridge, Wiltshire

Acknowledgements

The author would like to thank

- Mr Jack Knight of Mouchel for proofreading the text. Mr Knight is a leading expert on international marketing and acquisition, and gave a lot of sound advice (not all of which was accepted).
- Those people in the various consulting companies and international financing institutions for background conversations and advice.
- Those organisations who gave permission to quote from their publications, including

Asian Development Bank	IBC Conferences
Carl Hanser Verlag	New Civil Engineer
Deutsches Ingenieurblatt	OPEC Fund for International
European Bank for	Development
Reconstruction and	Overseas Development
Development	Administration
EU Phare	The Economist
Fédération Internationale	World Bank
Des Ingénieurs-Conseils	

- The author's editor, Ms Sally Smith, for her patience.

The author would also like to thank his wife, for her continuing intelligent and common-sense advice.

Any mistakes in the text are the author's own.

Contents

List of tables   xi

List of figures   xiii

Chapter 1 Introduction   **1**

Who this book is meant for   2
Structure of the book   2
First ideas   4

Chapter 2 Marketing (1)   **6**

What is marketing?   6
Marketing and international proposals   6
The difference between marketing, project
   acquisition and selling   6
The difference between company representative,
   regional director, acquisiteur, salesman, engineer   7

Who does the marketing?   8
Engineers or salesmen   8
Local office or international HQ   8
Do or die local office   9
Local associate company   10
Desktop marketing   10
Butterfly salesman   10
Summary   11

Marketing strategies   11
Shotgun marketing   12
Sharpshooter marketing   12
The two-month strategy   13
The blindfold approach   13
Summary   13

Developing a marketing strategy 14
  Why you need a marketing strategy 14
  Questions your strategy should answer 14
  Steps in developing a marketing strategy 16

Marketing basics 18
  Client awareness 20
  Types of project information 20
  Sources of project information 21

Summary 26

Chapter 3 Invitation **28**

The formal way of getting an invitation 28
  Three-stage consultant selection 28
  Start: client announces details of a new project 29
  First stage selection: expressions of interest 31
  Second stage: pre-qualification documents 34
  Third stage: proposals 37

Other ways of getting an invitation 37
  Short cuts 37
  Why clients sometimes use short cuts in selecting
    consultants 39

Consultants' own project selection procedure 40
  Two levels of selection 40

Chapter 4 Registrations **43**

General 43
  What is registration? 43
  Who and what do you register? 46
  Who do you register with? 47
  What information do you register? 47
  Summary 48

Examples of registration systems 49
  General 49
  Overseas Development Administration 50
  European Bank for Reconstruction and Development 52
  United Nations 52
  EU Phare 54
  European Commission 56
  DACON (Data on CONsultants) 56
  European Investment Bank 57

Advantages and disadvantages of the registration system   58
    Summary   61

Chapter 5 Proposals' preparation   **63**

Overview of preparing a proposal   63
    Three phases and eight stages   64

Preliminary review   64
    Terms of reference   65
    Task definition   67
    Background research   69
    Introduction to evaluation systems   71
    Project staff   73
    Project partners   73
    Decisions   74
    Summary: the preliminary review   75

Start-up   75
    Proposals team   76
    Proposals programme   81
    Proposals office   88
    Proposals budget   89

Brainstorming meeting   91

Site visit   93

Reducing the costs of proposals   94
    Proposals team   94
    Proposals programme   95
    Proposals budget   95
    Proposals office   95
    Brainstorming meeting   96
    Site visit   97
    Summary   97

Chapter 6 Writing technical proposals   **99**

Introduction   99
    Techniques   99
    Methodology   100
    Administration   102
    Style notes   103

Technical proposal structure and contents   106

The main sections of the technical proposal   109
    Section 1. Title page   110

Section 2. Submission letter 112
Section 3. Table of contents 114
Section 4. Introduction 116
Section 5. Company description 119
Section 6. Site appreciation 124
Section 7. Project appreciation 125
Section 8. Approach and methodology (1) – task lists 127
Section 9. Approach and methodology (2) – technical notes 131
Section 10. Approach and methodology (3) – key themes 134
Section 11. Work programme 136
Section 12. Comments on the TOR 144
Section 13. Staff CVs 146
Section 14. Association arrangements 149
Section 15. Estimates of local facilities 154
Section 16. Appendices/other material 157

Summary 158
Summary—writing technical proposals 158

Chapter 7   Writing financial proposals **160**

Introduction 160
Basic techniques 162
Understanding the problem 162
Software/spreadsheets 166
Twin documents 167
Sources of information 168
Financial proposals team 169
Time to prepare the financial proposal 170
Document administration 170

Financial proposal structure and contents 170

The main sections of the financial proposal 172
Background notes 174
Remuneration: 1. Basic salaries 176
Remuneration: 2. Social charges 178
Remuneration: 3. Overhead costs 180
Remuneration: 4. Fee mark-up 182
Out-of-pocket expenses: 5. Per diem 183
Out-of-pocket expenses: 6. Transport 185
Out-of-pocket expenses: 7. Accommodation 188
Out-of-pocket expenses: 8. Equipment 190
Out-of-pocket expenses: 9. Insurance and taxes 191
Out-of-pocket expenses: 10. Administration 193
Summary: 11. Summary table 195
12. Contingencies 195

Appendices/other material   196
Summary   197
    Summary—writing financial proposals   197

Chapter 8   Comparisons   **198**

Introduction   198
Business comparison   198
Technical QA   199
Style QA   199
General   201
Summary   201

Chapter 9   Submission   **202**

Introduction   202
Document production   202
Document submission   203
Cleaning up   205
Summary   205

Chapter 10   Signing contracts   **206**

Preparation   206
Negotiations   206
Bribery   206
Safety nets   207
Signing contracts   207
Summary   207

Chapter 11   Follow-up/Marketing (2)   **209**

Importance of the technical proposal   209
Follow-up   211
Marketing (2)   212
Summary   212

Chapter 12   References   **213**

Introduction   213
Project references   213
Staff references (CVs)   215
Development of references   216
Improving references   218
Other types of reference   222
Summary   223

Chapter 13 Discussion   **224**

What clients dislike about consultants   224
What consultants dislike about clients   225

Chapter 14 Summary   **228**

Important points to remember   228
Things that go wrong with proposals (and projects)   229

Chapter 15 Check lists   **231**

1. Consultants' own project selection procedures   232
2. Proposals team   233
3. Site visit questions   234
4. Technical proposals—basic details   235
5. Structure and content of the technical proposal   236
6. Items covered by the financial proposal
    Level 1—Remuneration   238
7. Items covered by the financial proposal
    Level 1—Out-of-pocket expenses (a)   240
8. Items covered by the financial proposal
    Level 1—Out of pocket expenses (b)   242
9. Structure and content of the financial proposal   244
10. Notes for people working overseas for the first time   245
11. Contents of project references   246
12. Contents of staff references   247

A1 Definitions   **248**
A2 Suggested reading   **257**

List of tables

1. Who does the marketing?   11
2. Marketing strategies   13
3. Questions to ask when developing a marketing strategy   17
4. Reliability of sources of project information   21
5. Sample list of contacts in the Czech Republic   22
6. Three-stage consultant selection   29
7. Examples of bank publications   30
8. Details to include in a letter (expression) of interest   32
9. Time and cost of preparing an EOI   33
10. Details to include in a PQ   35
11. Time and cost of preparing a PQ   37
12. Some comments on registration   45
13. Some details of the ODA registration form   50
14. Some examples of UN-related institutions   53
15. Summary notes on registration methods applied by some
    banks   58
16. Advantages and disadvantages of the registration system   61
17. Three phases and eight stages in writing a proposal   64
18. Information typically supplied with the Terms of Reference   66
19. Examples of formal evaluation systems for technical
    proposals   72
20. Example of evaluation points for key personnel   73
21. Members of the new proposals team   78
22. Brief characteristics of members of the old out-of-date
    proposals team   82
23. Costs of preparing a proposal   90
24. Income from a successful project   91
25. Time spent on the task-based approach using two different
    frameworks   102
26. Presentation and content   104
27. Structure and content of the technical proposal   108

28. One possible structure for company description   122
29. Example of a structured task list   128
30. Total months of service (work and leave)   140
31. Costs to client   140
32. Examples of local facilities (a) local support staff 155
33. Examples of local facilities (b) local equipment   155
34. Technical proposal—summary of chapter priorities   158
35. Technical proposal—amount of effort to be spent on each
    chapter   159
36. Elements of the financial proposal (examples)   164
37. Structure and content of the financial proposal   173
38. Key backstopping points   218
39. Contents of project references   219
40. Contents of staff references   220

List of figures

1. Steps in preparing an international proposal   3
2. One example of a strategy statement   19
3. Effects of the frequency of visits   25
4. Steps in developing a marketing strategy   26
5. Formal and informal consultant selection procedures   41
6. Value of registrations   60
7. Pressure and efficiency in preparing proposals   85
8. Overview of the proposals programme   87
9. Proposals preparation   97
10. Elements in the work programme   139
11. Core team staffing schedule—variations   140
12. Association arrangements   152
13. Main elements of the financial proposal   165
14. Sample financial table   167
15. Comparison and QA checks   200
16. Document submission   204
17. Signing contracts   208
18. Importance of the technical proposal   210
19. Comparative time spent on the technical proposal   211
20. References   221
21. Development of references   221

1

Introduction

Once upon a time, engineering consultants could set up an office, put a brass plate on the front door, and wait for custom. Hopeful clients would knock on the door. Entering the offices, cap in hand, they would humbly ask the consultant if he would provide them with his knowledge and skills. The customer would be happy to pay whatever fee was asked; and the consultants, unwilling to involve themselves with such lesser matters as *business*, agreed between themselves sets of fees for services provided. This is how the consulting profession began.

Those days are over now, and the world is none the worse for it. Consultants have to go round knocking on clients' doors. The clients themselves may not be skilled engineers but they are experts in their own area of interest, whether it is running a supermarket chain or heading the contracts department of an international financing institute. They are certainly hard-nosed businessmen, prepared to pay a high price for rare services — but certainly not for what have become the very common services offered by many consultants. In order to tempt prospective clients into employing them, consultants now have to offer an interesting package of skills at a competitive price. The way they do this is by writing a **proposal**. Such a document may once have been little more than a brief letter accompanied by one or two CVs. It now covers a hundred or more pages of notes and calculations, and as much text as a small gothic novel.

This book is a guide on how to write proposals. It suggests how you should go about the task, and how you should not. One thing it does *not* do is tell you exactly what to do for every proposal you may have to work on. Every football players knows the basics of the game but has to make his own decisions during each game. So will you have to make your own decisions during each proposal. If this wasn't the case, even your secretary could write the thing.

Who this book is meant for

The most important readers of the book will be engineers — mainly because engineers are the people who usually end up having to write the proposals. Modern consultancies have a second group of experts whose involvement in proposals is just as important as that of the technical experts. They are the businessmen. Sometimes more sensitively described as a 'company representative', 'regional director', 'marketing expert' or 'acquisiteur', the businessman is the person who probably knows most about the client and what he really wants (compared with what the documents say he wants). Managers of modern engineering consultancies will also find useful material in this book. They will want to find ways of reducing the cost of preparing proposals, and of solving problems which the writers may be faced with. They will also want to know whether it is worthwhile writing the proposal in the first place. Company accountants should be involved in, at least, the preparation of the financial proposal. They will want to know what role they have to play, and why. Project managers are the people who have to plan (and fight for) the allocation of resources for both the project and the work on the proposal documents. The book will support their arguments in both cases. Last, but not least, students reading the book may begin to understand that the modern engineer has two main tasks in life: successfully completing the project currently being worked on, and working to win the next one.

Structure of the book

The main phases involved in writing a proposal are

- being asked to write one
- preparation
- writing the proposal
- submitting it
- signing contracts
- following up the work

and the main chapters of the book follow these phases (Fig. 1). There are also two additional subjects which are as important to a successful and cost-effective proposal as any engineering input. Marketing is where the businessman convinces the client of the skills and seriousness of his company. This leads up to the invitation to submit a proposal; well-prepared reference material can save the businessman and the proposal authors both time and money.

When you have to work on a particular task, it is worth beginning with some idea or outline of what you are trying to do. The book has a number of check lists to help you develop these outlines and specifies some of the more interesting tasks in preparing and writing international proposals.

Before discussing marketing, it would be worth clearing up some first ideas on international proposals, such as which technical disciplines and countries they cover.

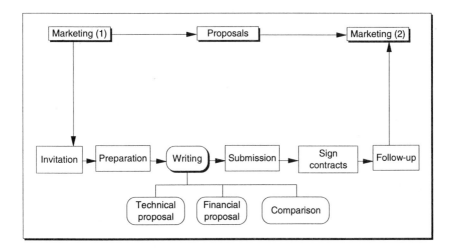

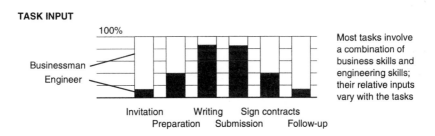

TASK INPUT

Most tasks involve a combination of business skills and engineering skills; their relative inputs vary with the tasks

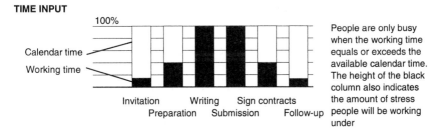

TIME INPUT

People are only busy when the working time equals or exceeds the available calendar time. The height of the black column also indicates the amount of stress people will be working under

Fig. 1. Steps in preparing an international proposal

First ideas

International proposals cover many disciplines These days even a simple rural road design project is a major multi-disciplinary task. Company representatives have to provide background knowledge on local rules and regulations; geologists will advise on likely sources of construction material; environmentalists will help with the route selection; sociologists will give advice on how to resettle local populations whose homes or businesses will be in the pathway of the new road, and accountants will provide figures on company overheads, staff costs and reimbursables. You may also need to use the services of more unusual disciplines, such as bomb disposal and mine clearance teams or airport installations experts. If you are not used to multi-disciplinary work, or don't like talking to urban planners or environmentalists, then don't get involved in proposals.

International proposals cover many companies It is a rare company (or company group) that has all these skills within it; besides, many international financing institutions (IFIs) or banks insist on some element of technology transfer during the consultancy services. To do this you need someone to transfer the technology to. This is one reason for including a local consulting company in your proposed study team, which in turn means the proposal comes from more than one company.

International proposals cover new projects in many countries — including the UK. Many of the joint venture groups competing for some of the UK's recent Build Operate Transfer (BOT) road projects included consultants from a number of other countries. Companies often have to prepare proposals for major new projects in their own country in the same way they would do if the proposals were for a project abroad.

International clients are not just the banks Some companies believe that the money for the more interesting international projects come from international financing agencies such as the World Bank, and that these are therefore their *clients of first interest* (usually meaning, they can forget everyone else). This is wrong for two reasons: first, the banks usually fund schemes proposed by others, such as national or regional governments; second, private developers and private banks (etc) can also sponsor schemes which need the consultant's services. If you concentrate your marketing efforts on the banks alone, you will immediately lose half the projects.

Any company can be an international consultant The term no longer applies only to major consultancy groups with offices in several countries. After all, the simplest definition of an international consultant is someone (or some company) who has worked abroad at some time. If your company is small but has worked on a project in France, then it has as much right to be considered an *international consultant* as a group with ten offices in South-East Asia and 1200 employees. It also has as much right to compete for international proposals as anyone else.

Regions, groups and sectors Tailor-made suits are designed to fit the target client's specific measurements — waist, chest, neck and so on. Tailor-made proposals focus on their target client's measurements of region, group and sector, where

- *region* is the geographical location of the project (e.g. South-East Asia, Central Europe)
- *group* describes the type of client (central government, private developer)
- *sector* refers to the technical discipline which the new project will involve (road construction, water supply, urban development etc.)

There are two measures of time Managers and other people often reasonably ask engineers how long it will take them to do a particular task. They may need to prepare a proposal for a second project, for example. The engineer may say that it will take him a week; but he may mean either that

(*a*)   it will take one calendar week to complete the task (he expects to wait two days before he obtains some important data, the work will take him three days full-time, and he doesn't intend to work during the weekend) — this is one week of *calendar* time

(*b*)   it will take seven full working days of the engineer's own time to complete the task (including the weekend) — but it may take longer if he doesn't receive the data soon — this is one week of his own, of *working* time.

So far as proposals are concerned, problems often arise when the engineer means (*b*) and the manager understands him to mean (*a*), or vice versa.

2

Marketing (1)

What is marketing?

Marketing and international proposals

It is possible that a prospective client finds your company details in the *yellow pages* of his local phone directory and calls you to invite your company to submit a proposal for a major new project — just. But these occasions are rare; and international clients won't even have a copy of your local phone directory.

Usually your company will have to invest time, money and effort in order to receive such invitations. This is what marketing is about. Usually

- marketing leads to an invitation to submit a proposal for the new project
- a successful proposal leads to the client awarding your company the project
- a successful project gives you more material for the next round of marketing activity.

The difference between marketing, project acquisition and selling

One explanation of these terms is that *marketing* is the act of spreading awareness of the company's skills and services, *project acquisition* is the drama of winning a new contract for consultancy services, while *selling* is something which shop assistants and door-to-door brush retailers do. Engineers and consultants invoke a variety of terms like these, when they are usually talking about the same thing — selling. They avoid using the 's' word partly because it has a certain stigma attached to it, as if it is not an activity which people with university degrees and professional qualifications do for a living. In fact, everyone is a salesman. The bridge engineering graduate who is applying for his first job is selling himself. Children who talk their parents into buying them ice-creams have just completed a sale. Even proposing to your future spouse is a determined act of salesmanship. Selling is a constructive, useful and universally practiced activity, and the successful salesman has something to be proud of — whether he is an engineer or an assistant at Boots' cosmetic counter.[1]

There is one other reason why engineers void the 's' word, and that is because selling implies hard work and hard planning. Marketing, however, has an image of business dinners, meetings with leading politicians, and the occasional appearance on a business TV programme — which sounds much more fun. In fact marketing, project acquisition and selling mean the same thing. They cover the second of the modern engineer's two main tasks: successfully completing the current project, *and winning the next one.*

The difference between company representative, regional director, acquisiteur, salesman, engineer

Terms like these can mean different things in different companies. In conventional consultancies they can imply a hierarchy of roles, each narrowly defined, and a top – down approach to the management of projects. Conventional engineers like the terms because they give a certain status and because, as an *engineer* they can get on and do the work they studied so hard to learn. The modern engineer realises that the roles have very much in common. Whether director, representative or engineer they have to produce high quality products for their existing clients while at the same time keeping an eye out for new ones. All the roles have the one task in common — selling.[2] Perhaps this should lead to a change in consultancies' internal structures — fewer levels in the hierarchy, on the lines of 'those who can, do; those who can't, should no longer be employed with the company'; or project-based virtual teams. Consultants sell people and not products. They need more people with the ability to do things themselves, fewer people whose sole skill is their ability to tell others what to do.

---

1   for one introduction to the art of selling, see Tom Hopkins' *How to master the art of selling.* Further reference details of this and other books are given in Appendix A2.

2   *Re-engineering the corporation* by Hammer & Champy (appendix A2) still makes interesting reading (the theory has a better reputation than the practice).

Who does the marketing?

The question is relevant to writing proposals, since the method your company uses can affect the quality and accessibility of the local information you will need. There are various answers to the question, but not all will be suited to every firm. For example, one answer is for a company to set up a local office in each country it is interested in; this method will not be available if your own company has only two employees. Various other possibilities are explored below.

Engineers or salesmen

Once upon a time salesmen sold and engineers engineered — at least in theory. The dividing line has all but disappeared now. Suppose you are an engineer and as *client* want to buy an expensive new computer to run the latest highway design software. You would expect the salesman who greets you to tell you more about the machine than that 'it is PC compatible and can run Windows'. If you are a highway engineer then the salesman should be able to discuss the computer's compatibility with MOSS and Intergraph highway design packages, and otherwise know something about what you as an engineer will be expecting it to do.

In the same way, the salesman (or representative) who markets your company should know a considerable amount about the product the client has shown interest in. If the client is interested in tunnels and asks whether the opencast or NATM (new Austrian tunnelling method) approach would be better, he would hope for a more positive response from the salesman than 'I'll have to ask my head office'.

From your company's point of view, a representative who knows something about what he is trying to sell is useful. He will be better able to spot the potentially interesting project from the background static of general conversation and information.

Local office or international HQ

Company representatives (whatever their background) can work from the firm's international headquarters or from a local office. Both have advantages and disadvantages. The advantage of running the marketing from a local office is that you can develop and maintain a network of good local contacts. These will provide you with high-quality background on possible new projects almost as soon as they are thought of. The disadvantage is the cost. Your company will also have to pay for the representative's salary and that of a local secretary, plus the costs of an office and personal accommodation. If the representative is an engineer then he may be able to offset the local office overheads by carrying out small local projects himself — although this will leave him less time for marketing.

If your company's head office does the international marketing, then the representatives will be closer to the firm's policy-makers and engineering experts. He will be better able to tell the policy-makers how the market is developing, and better able to tell the clients of the new products and skills which the experts can offer. However, the speed and quality of the project information he can provide will be lower. Your company will still have to pay the representative's salary, provide him with support staff and office space, plus pay travel and hotel costs for the regular marketing visits he will have to make to the country.

Companies may be reluctant to open a local office until they have won a project in the country (which will offset some of the local office costs). This sounds a bit like the person who wouldn't write a book until he had a word processor, but couldn't afford the word processor until he'd earned some money from his first book.

One leading consultant has an interesting viewpoint on this subject

> Working overseas . . . now it is almost impossible to win contracts without having an office in the country and using local staff [3]

Do or die local office

One American-style way of starting up a local office, is to send out a trusted member of the company with the instruction that he has a year to make a success of the local office: if he is unsuccessful he will be fired. The disadvantage with this method is that the representative will concentrate more on marketing himself than the company — so preparing a safety net for himself if the local office doesn't make a profit. He is also likely to keep overheads down by taking fewer risks. The method is not one which will foster goodwill and trust between the head office and the representative; and representatives who do not have dependable backstopping support will survive like plants without water.

3   W. S. Atkins chief executive, Michael Jeffries, quoted in Helena Russell's article 'High Profile', New Civil Engineer Consultants File, April 1996.

Local associate company

Teaming up with a local company in the country of interest can save your firm time and money. It can also provide an instant network of contacts and a high-quality source of background information. There are preconditions of course. The first one is that you have to be able to offer the local company something in return. This could be a potential for projects in your own country, staff with special skills which they can use in their proposals, or a direct form of technology transfer to their own staff. Another precondition is that you must be able to trust the local company (and they you). Without this you run the risk of your local partner using your information and ideas for their own sole gain. You can even risk damaging your company's good name (picture the headlines 'local firm accused of bribing officials — "our London associate had nothing to do with it" claims director').

   If your company does decide to work with a local firm, it cannot leave the responsibility for maintaining contacts to someone from its own senior management. Such people usually have neither the time nor the detailed knowledge to do the job properly.

Desktop marketing

This is the exercise whereby the international projects department staff scan business journals and bank publications for news of a likely new project. For every likely scheme they spot, they send away a company brochure and a letter saying that their firm would be delighted to carry out the work. Their chances of success are as high as the chance of someone finding the perfect spouse through the lonely hearts column of the local newspaper — not impossible, but not something to bet your future on. Not least of the problems with bank and business journals is that they are at best *secondary* sources of project information, which means that they are possibly incomplete, incorrect and certainly out-of-date. (The *primary* source of project information is the person who is promoting it.) Full-time, desktop marketing can degenerate into a means of wasting money in an apparently purposeful way.

Butterfly salesman

The butterfly flits from flower to flower, pausing for an instant to collect some refreshing nectar and then passing on to the next one. Some representatives (and even senior management) tend to act like this when they are marketing for their company. They call in on country A for a five-minute meeting with one potential client's senior staff, then fly off to country B for a five-minute meeting with a senior representative of a possible client there, and so on. Clients treated in this way are likely to make complimentary remarks about the representative and his company — clients after all can be as polite as the next man — but they won't treat them seriously. Just as this isn't a serious way for you to market your company.

Summary

There are certainly other ways of having someone market and sell your company, but the rule in each case must be to think before you act. You should try and work out the advantages and disadvantages (the costs and likely rewards) of each method. Meanwhile Table 1 gives a subjective evaluation of the marketing methods discussed above. The table suggests that if you are an engineer involved in desktop marketing then your chances of success are small — but at least you won't get caught out in the rain.

Marketing strategies

Suppose you agree that your company should begin with some sort of a marketing strategy: you still have to decide what type of strategy you want to use, and what its main points are to be. There are at least four types of strategy you can choose from: *shotgun, marksman, blindfold* and the *two-month strategy*.

Table 1. *Who does the marketing?*

Type	Quality of technical information	Speed of reply	Cost	Value
Travelling salesman	Poor	Poor	Minimal	5
Travelling engineer	Good	Poor	Minimal	7
Local office	Good	Good	Medium	6
International HQ	Fair	Poor	Medium	5
Do or die local office	Fair	Fair	High	5
Local associate/management contacts	Poor	Poor	Minimal	5
Local associate/engineer contacts	Good	Fair	Minimal	8
Desktop marketing	Poor	Poor	High	3
Butterfly salesmanship	Poor	Poor	High	3

* A higher score suggests better value.

Shotgun marketing

In the first type of strategy, your company decides to offer all possible services in every country in the world. You can do this whether your company is a two-engineer outfit or has 200 specialists. After all, even the smaller companies can offer every specialist service on the grounds that 'I can't do it myself, but I know someone who can'. The logic behind this approach is that if you chase after every possible project then your chances of winning at least one must be very high. There are two explanations as to why it doesn't work — the reasoned and the mathematical.

First, the reasoned explanation. Consider the case of a bridge design engineer who is looking for a new job. He could send off a copy of his CV to every kitchen and swimming-pool design consultant in Britain, but they would be unlikely to invite him to an interview; after all, he does not have the relevant experience. The bridge engineer could also broadcast his career details to prospective employers in Angola and North-West Cambodia; but a moment's reflection should suggest that the risks would be presently too high for him to accept a job in these countries. What makes sense for a single engineer also makes sense for an engineering consultancy.

Now, the mathematical explanation. Suppose that

- a company works in ten main technical sectors (e.g. highway design, environmental studies)
- there are 170 countries in the world
- its international department has four representatives
- there are 200 working days in the year.

This means that the company has 1700 marketing opportunities and 800 working days a year to market them in — something less than four hours a year (without allowing for tea-breaks). Even concentrating on just one sector allows the representatives less than five days per country per year.

The normal minimum time for one trip to one country is five days (unless you have a secretary to do the preparation and forget about the debriefing)

○ 1 day preparation	○ 1 day return travel, plus
○ 1 day travel	○ 1 day debriefing.
○ 1 day meetings	

Sharpshooter marketing

This approach requires taking aim at particular countries and at particular product areas which your company want to offer in them.

Table 2. Marketing strategies

Type	Time per client	Country Knowledge	Network Development	Value*
Shotgun marketing	Low	Poor	Poor	3
Sharpshooter marketing	High	Good	Good	9
The two-month strategy	High, for a brief period	Fair	Minimal	5
The blindfold approach	Minimal, if any	Minimal	None	0
No-strategy approach	Minimal	Minimal	None	0
Changeable strategy approach	Minimal	Minimal	None	0

* A higher score suggests better value.

It also means making a decision on what regions and products your company is *not* interested in, at least for the present. But it does give you much more time to make contacts, meet clients and learn about what the local market is looking for.

The two-month strategy

This is a managed version of sharpshooter marketing. Here your director gives you two months to bring in a project in a country that has just been given to you to develop. If you are not successful within this time the strategy will change and you will be given another region to market in. The problem here is that, *unless you have a very unusual product to offer*, it can take you at least a year to establish yourself with clients and contacts in a new country. Experienced engineers suggest it will take as much as two to three years to become successful in certain countries.

The blindfold approach

Here, your company has developed a new marketing strategy but its internal communications system doesn't work very well. You take off on a marketing trip without knowing what the latest version of the strategy is. One of the purposes of the ISO 9000 Quality Management system is to encourage companies to develop effective internal communications (both technical and personal). A variation on the blindfold approach is where your company doesn't have a marketing strategy at all.

Summary

Table 2 gives a subjective evaluation of the marketing strategies discussed above. The table suggests that a well-defined strategy is likely to have the best chance of success.

Developing a marketing strategy

Why you need a marketing strategy

A marketing strategy helps you to decide which projects are worth-while trying to acquire. Limited resources means that you cannot afford to chase after every project under the sun. It also tells you where the company plans to go in the future, since the marketing strategy is a core part of the company's corporate strategy. Your company needs a corporate/marketing strategy before it can begin to

- make decisions
- plan resources
- develop new products
- open or close offices
- institute staff training programmes
- outline financial and staff budgets for its marketing activities.

Questions your strategy should answer

Whatever strategy you develop should answer four basic questions.

Where do you want to market? Your company probably doesn't have the resources or local associates to market in every country and region in the world. Someone has to decide on priorities. It helps that some regions and countries are more potentially profitable than others, and some regions are high risk areas. You might, for example, be reluctant to assign one of your colleagues to a feasibility study in Ruanda. Siberia may make an interesting field assignment for a geological engineer, but some clients from the Russian Federation cannot pay their bills — the area is a high risk, at least in business terms. More direct considerations may be that your company wants to build on the considerable experience it has gained in the Middle East, or that it has several local offices in Germany.

Who do you want to market to? An engineering consultancy's international department has many potential clients. Now and again one particular group becomes the flavour of the month, so that every consultancy bombards them with company brochures. In the UK in the 1970s it was local government, in the 1980s private developers; at the moment the IFIs are tops. Without a marketing strategy your company may lose themselves in the herd and only sell to the same targets as everyone else.

Identifying potential clients also has something to do with what services you want to offer. For example, you could find that your building services department has more potential clients among architectural firms and private development companies than it can hope to find through contacting international banks.

What do you want to market? Your company's marketing strategy should also define some sort of priority for the products and services it can offer. If your company's environmental department has just two graduates with one year's experience between them, whereas the bridge engineering department has 200 chartered engineers, then perhaps your priority should be to find projects that involve structures. Offering clients whatever services they want may be a good idea at times; but if your company doesn't have the necessary skills it will have to team up with another company — and this is where your company's profit begins to disappear.

When deciding what to market you will want to listen to the advice of the specialist engineering departments (as they should want to listen to the advice of the people who work in the marketing department). You should also consider your company's perceived services as well as its own practical services and products. Your marketing strategy should at least include reference to one or two new services, so that you can show potential clients that you are moving with the times. You cannot sell old goods in old markets — these days it is difficult even to sell old goods in new markets. Examples of these product and service types are

- *own products*: company-developed pavement management software
- *conventional services*: expertise in MOSS software or in the design of concrete structures
- *perceived services*: your company's reputation for integrity; Germany's reputation for high-quality engineering
- *new services*: such as GIS-T — Geographic Information System is a new, computer-based method for multi-disciplinary area-wide projects and GIS-T is the branch of GIS which covers transportation-related studies — and multi-disciplinary urban studies (having an Internet address does not constitute a new service).

Who markets what? There is nothing more embarrassing than for two people from the same company to market their firm to the same potential client. Your marketing strategy should make clear who is supposed to be responsible for what. If Mr. Johnson is to be responsible for the Singapore and Malaysia markets, then everyone in the company — from the managing director down — has to speak with Mr. Johnson before making a sales visit to these countries. This is one case where information exchange is not two-way. Mr. Johnson's local contacts are valuable assets, and have to be protected from abuse; putting their details on the company database will only encourage someone else to call them directly.

Steps in developing a marketing strategy

If your company already has a sound marketing strategy then all you have to do is to start applying it. Alternatively, if you question whether the current strategy really fits the modern world you might well want to revise it. Points which you should then consider include the questions in Table 3 and Fig. 2.

In practice, some clients will be more interested in one range of services than another. Architects' for example, might be more interested in building access and parking capacity than in railway engineering services. Some regions will have a different range of potential clients than in others; consultants would not expect to find many private developers in communist countries. This means that you will have to carry out some sort of multi-dimensional market analysis, of

- region/country *against* types of client *against* products and services.

The result will give an idea of priorities as well as favoured services and clients etc. The examples in Table 3 suggest that one marketing target with a triple-A rating might be 'network management services for private developers in Malaysia', while one with a bottom, triple-C rating would be 'highway design for central government in Angola'.

The marketing budget and other resources Developing a marketing strategy in this way will suggest priorities but even so it has so far only addressed half the problem. Suppose you or your company management have developed a strategy which lists 40 priority groups in 20 countries. To implement this strategy your company has set up an international department with two full-time engineers (one of which is you) and an annual budget equalling around US$10 000 a year. Immediately two things become clear

- there's not enough money in the budget to pay you and your colleague's salaries, let alone travel and accommodation expenses
- you have time for about two days' direct client/country group contacts each year[4] (without allowing any time to actually write any proposals).

---

4 Five days per visit including travel — 20 country/client groups per person — 200 working days a year.

Table 3 (below and overleaf).   Questions to ask when developing a marketing strategy

Positive questions	Negative questions
Deciding which regions and countries	
Which regions and countries does your company have experience in?	Which regions/countries can you rule out because they are too dangerous?
Which countries do your company's professional staff have experience in?	Which countries can you rule out because they are financially too risky?
Which countries does your company have an office in?	Which countries do you not really stand a chance at all in (e.g. Japan, USA)?
Which regions/countries does your company have a local associate company in?	Which regions/countries are in a financial recession at the moment (e.g. the Middle East; Saudi Arabia)?
Which regions/countries does your own country have useful connections with (e.g. Hong Kong for the UK; Turkey for Germany)?	Which regions/countries will it cost most to market in (e.g. South-East Asia)?
Which regions/countries are developing rapidly?	
Which regions/countries will it cost least to market in (e.g. Western and Central Europe)?	

Answers to these questions will begin to give you a weighting system for countries of interest. For example, (A=good, C=poor)

A = UK	(why ignore all that pooled local knowledge)
A = Malaysia	(rapid growth rate from a comparatively low base)
B = Saudi Arabia	(it is still developing and there is still potential for the right services)
C = Angola	(it is still a dangerous area)

Deciding which clients	
Which clients does your company already have (perhaps local government)?	Which types of client is everyone else chasing after?
Which types of client has your company experience of working with (e.g. private developer)?	With which types of client do you have no chance at all?
Which types of client have your professional colleagues experience of working with (e.g. central government)?	Which client groups are presently short of funds (e.g. central government)?

Examples of weightings
A = private developer
B = state-owned industry (no information yet)
C = central government

Positive questions	Negative questions
Deciding which services	
Which products and services does your company already have?	Which traditional engineering services have become low technology products (e.g. highway design)?
Which types of product has your company experience of working with?	Which services really have no future at all (e.g. design of nuclear power stations)?
Which services have your professional colleagues experience of working with?	
What sort of services do your target client groups say they want?	
What sort of services do your target client groups really need?	
What can you imagine the services of the future to be?	

A = network management
B = Global Positioning System (GPS)-fleet management
C = highway design

Your company management will have to cut the marketing strategy to fit the cloth (resources) it is prepared to provide. One rule-of-thumb is that it can take 1–2 years' calendar time, six months' working time and US$100 000[5] to open up a new market.

One other point on marketing strategy Once your company has developed a strategy, start implementing it. You will then find that some of its basic premises are wrong. The country of choice may be going through a recession, or the potential client is more interested in managing his existing roads rather than in building new ones. A marketing strategy is meant to be a guide for wise men, not instructions for fools.

Marketing basics

The whole point of developing and applying a marketing strategy is to identify potential clients, find out what they want to do, and

5   At $10 000 per month staff costs plus travel, accommodation and other knowledge acquisition expenses.

(eventually) help them to do it. This doesn't mean that, once you have developed a strategy, you immediately apply it by knocking on the first client's door and handing out company brochures. It will help if you learn something about the client first, and if you can find out some useful information about possible new projects.

Where do you want to market?

Region	Priority	Reasons
Central Europe*	A	
Western Europe†	A	
China‡	A	
South-East Asia§	A	
Mediterranean rim	B	Low in funds presently
Middle East	C	Recession area
Russian Federation	C	Financially risky
South America	C	Unknown potential
Antarctica	—	Not populated
Australasia	—	Self-sufficient
Eastern Europe	—	Financially risky
India	—	Unknown potential
Japan	—	Self-sufficient
North America	—	Self-sufficient
Southern Africa	—	Low in funds

*Central Europe in detail

Country	Priority	Reasons
Poland	A	Best local knowledge
Czech Rep.	A	
Hungary	B	
Slovenia	C	Lack of funds
Slovakia	—	
Rumania	—	

†Western Europe in detail

Country	Priority	Reasons
Germany	A	Best local knowledge
France	B	
Italy	B	EU railway schemes
Turkey	B	EU development area
UK	B	Developing railways
Greece	C	
Sweden	—	
Denmark	—	

Who do you want to market to?

Potential clients **	Priority	Reasons
Private developers	A	For specialist services
EU	A	Major source of funds
IFIs	B	Often secondary sources
Local government	B	Scope for new services
Private banks	B	Growing BOT sponsors
Private industry	B	Scope for new services
Central government	C	Lack of funds
State-owned industry	C	Conservative

** ranking varies from country to country

‡China in detail

Province	Priority	Reasons
Henan	A	Rapidly developing
Xian	B	
Hong Kong	—	

§South-East Asian in detail

Country	Priority	Reasons
Indonesia	A	Large market
Malaysia	A	Rapidly developing
Phillipines	B	Early development
Vietnam	B	Everyone else is there
Laos	B	Small market
Cambodia	C	Staff risk

What do you want to market?

Own products	Conventional services	Perceived services
(none)	Highway design	International reputation
	Highway maintenance	Years of in-country experience
	Bridge design	
	Bridge maintenance	
	Urban planning	**New services**
	Development studies	GIS-T
	Architectural design	Urban studies
	Building installations	Pavement management
	Structural design	Network management
	Structural maintenance	Remote sensing
	Railway engineering	

Fig. 2. One example of a strategy statement (key to weightings, A = good, C = poor)

Client awareness

The less successful salesman is the type who tries to sell newspaper subscriptions to someone who can't read. You have to be aware of what potential clients try to do and how they try to do it. Suppose an engineering consultancy had an interest in expanding into France and Belgium. It might decide to send a marketing representative to visit the European Bank for Reconstruction and Development (EBRD) as often as once every four weeks. Despite the time and expense this would cost the company, its chances of winning a major project would be low, since the EBRD is only concerned with projects in Central and Eastern Europe.

To take another example, a consultancy with a large drainage design division might be interested in winning a project for a new residential area drainage network in the Gulf State of Qatar. The firm should be aware of one major point before they write to the Ministry of Municipal Affairs in Doha. Qatar has perhaps the world's most advanced urban GIS system. As early as 1993, drainage engineers could call up closed circuit television and photo images of existing drainage lines through their GIS. Any expression of interest for the new drainage design project should at least make some constructive reference to the technique.

Types of project information

There are various types of project information, and various sources which can provide you with it. Different sources will give different types of information. The main types are

- *early and late information*: the difference between these is that one gives you information *before* the client awards the contract; the other comes from a source who excitedly passes on the first news of the scheme two days *after* the contract award
- *background information*: it is usually not enough to know that Berlin is planning to build a new airport. What you would also like to know are answers to questions such as

  - Who is the head of the subcommittee responsible for the project?
  - Has the initial feasibility study been done?
  - Which building/financing companies have expressed an interest in the scheme?
  - What is the likely timetable of development of the project?

   °   Who really makes the political and who makes the engineering decisions on the project?

Sources of project information

There are different sources of project information, each with its own degree of reliability (Table 4). For example, would you assume the following sources are as reliable as each other

(a)   a junior engineer in the client's office who tells you that the the company will only award the scheme to a French engineering consultancy, or

(b)   the director who tells you the company will award it to the lowest European bidder.

Potential sources of project information include

- *client management*: as reliable as is your personal relationship with them, but capable of giving early and informal background details of new schemes
- *client engineer*: usually knows more about the technical background to the scheme and the various arguments for and against its implementation; also likely to know who will really be making the decision about consultant selection, as opposed to who the client says will make the decision
- *Bank journals*: can provide you with out-of-date information; for example, subscribers to the EBRD's *Procurement Opportunities* may read about some technical cooperation projects only after the closing date for expressions of interest in them (they are first advertised in the Bank's fax information service); and details of Asian Development Bank (ADB) projects often appear first in their Internet site

Table 4.   *Reliability of sources of project information*

Potential source	Likely reliability	Early	Late	Background	Value*
		Type of information			
Client management	Fair	x		Fair	6
Client engineer	Good	x		Good	7
IFI journals	Fair to poor		x	–	1
Government-based journals	Poor		x	–	0
Embassies	Fair		x	Fair	4
Regional or theme journals	Good	x		Some	4
Personal contacts	Very good	x		Good	8

* A higher score suggests better value.

Table 5. Sample list of contacts in the Czech Republic

EU Phare		Number of possible contacts
National coordinators		
National coordinator of official	Ministry (M.) of Economy	2
non-reimbursable foreign assets	Centre for Foreign Assistance (CFA)	1
Phare unit	Phare unit	2
G-24 unit	G-24 unit	2
GTAF–PMU	GTAF–PMU	5
European integration	Europe agreement — coordination of Phare assets	1
	Europe agreement — legislation	1
		14
National programmes		
Phare programme implementing agencies		
Agriculture	Agriculture — PMU (M. of Agriculture)	1
	Czech office for survey, mapping and cadaster	1
Civil society development	Civil society development foundation	3
Customs administration	General directorate of customs	2
Education, HR, training	Renewal of education programme — PMU (M. of Education)	3
	Pilot schools vocational training reform programme	2
	National Training Fund, Czech Republic	3
Energy	Energy — PMU (M. of Energy)	3
Enterprise restruct. & privat.	EXDEV — PMU (M. of Economy)	4
Environment	Environment — PMU (M. of Environment)	3
Finance and banking	Banking — Czech national bank	2
	Finance — PMU (M. of Finance)	3
Health	Ministry of Health, international department	3
Investment promotion etc	Czech agency for foreign investment	3
	Export promotion/restructuring (M. of Economy)	2
Nuclear safety	State office for nuclear safety	3
Public administration	Department for Public Administration	2
	Europe agreement — legislation (OLPA)	2
	Local government training foundation	1
Regional and local economic development	Ministry of Economy	1
	North Bohemia — regional development agency	2
	North Moravia — regional enterprise fund	4
	Regional development agency	3
Research and development	Czech Technical University	1
SME	SME — PMU (M. of Economy)	4
	Venture capital fund	1

EU Phare	Number of possible contacts	
	Venture capital fund, North Moravia	4
	Euro. info. centre network/ correspondence centre	1
Social policy and employment	Social programmes PMU	5
Statistics administration	Czech statistics office	4
Telecommunications	Telecommunications — PMU (M. of Economy)	1
	TestCom	3
Tourism	—	—
Transport	Transport — PMU (M. of Transport)	2
		82

Multi-country programmes (mcp)

Environment mcp	Black triangle PCU	2
	Danube PCU	1
Fight against drugs	National drug commission	1
Industrial property programme	Industrial property office	1
Standards/quality assurance	National programme — Czech office for standards etc.	1
ACE programme	Czech national bank, institute of economics	1
SIGMA	Office for legislation and public administration	1
	Financial policy department, M. of Finance	1
Transport	M. of Transport	2
		11

Other programmes

Cooperation in science and technology	Dept. of international cooperation (M. of Education)	2
Cross-border cooperation	Phare CBC (M. of Economy)	2
Phare JOPP programme	Investment and Postal Bank	2
		6

NGOs

Phare/Tacis democracy programme	(office)	2
TEMPUS	TEMPUS office	1
		3

European Commission delegations

	General	7
	Phare section	7
		14

Other international organisations

EBRD

Resident office	Resident office	2
Head office	Country team (Czech Republic, Slovak Republic, Hungary)	1
	Industry team	—
	Operational support units	—

UN

UN Economic Commission for Europe		1

Table 5. continued

World Bank International Financial Corporation (IFC) field representative		1
		5

Local organisations and institutions		
	Czech Institute for Traffic Engineering	1
	Czech Road Society	1
	Czech Roads Directorate	1
	Czech Standards Institute	1
		4
	total ~	140

The above list suggests the number of people that one large consulting company could consider as useful contacts, even in a comparatively small country like the Czech Republic.

*Phare originally stood for Poland and Hungary: assistance to the reconstruction of the economy, although the programme now covers more than just these two countries.

- *government-based journals*: also journals published by quangos; very often sources of second-hand, out-of-date information, whose main job may seem to be to provide employment for civil servants rather than a hot-off-the-press news delivery to private-sector consultants
- *Embassies*: can provide useful background information, provided the consultant has good personal contacts with someone in the Embassy's business section; otherwise as under government-based journals
- *regional or theme journals*: such as MEED (the *Middle East Economic Digest*) — the best ones give some background information plus regular updates which help you track the development of countries within the region and of new schemes within each country
- *personal contacts*: the best source — someone who knows you and your company well, and considers both to be reliable, competent, trustworthy and sensible. He will do his best to help you, and will tell you when (and why) he can't.

Developing personal contacts There is a certain skill in developing personal contacts. The basic requirement is that the marketing representative should be a pleasant and competent person. Beyond that, he should have some knowledge of the target country (the country where the consultant hopes to win a new project). This would help the representative identify which would be the most appropriate people and organisations for him to contact. In most cases the range

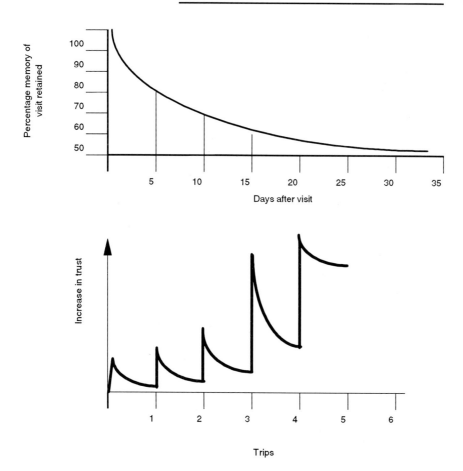

Fig. 3. Effects of the frequency of visits
Source: Marhold, Deutsches Ingenieurblatt, November 1995

of possibilities will be more than one person can sensibly handle (e.g. Table 5).

The marketing representative should also have a feeling for how often he should visit his contacts and potential clients. If he leaves too long a gap between visits, the client will have forgotten all about him and his company. Too short a gap, and the representative becomes a nuisance. A competing argument is that the trust that the client/ contact has in the representative increases with the number of visits made (Fig. 3). The representative has to work out the best answer for each client.

In most cases, the optimum frequency probably lies between one visit every 1–4 months (the maximum gap is probably the limit where opening a local office does become essential).

nary

(See also Fig. 4.)

- The modern engineer has two main tasks: successfully completing the current project, and winning the next one.
- Marketing and selling are a bit like gardening — you have to put in a lot of hard work before you see the first plants grow.
- You don't get inside information through circulars and press releases.
- Look on everyone in your company as a salesman, and everyone outside it as a client.

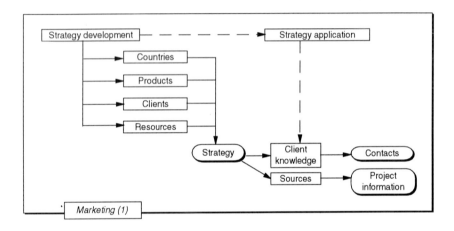

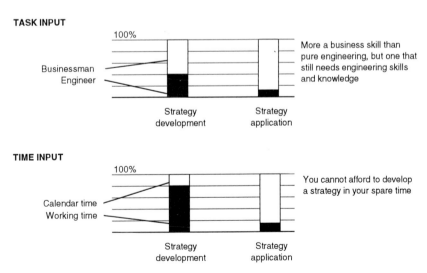

Fig. 4. Steps in developing a marketing strategy

- Ignorance of the client will score you minus points.
- Before approaching a potential new client (bank or government, developer or other consultancy) find out something about them first.
- Develop a marketing strategy and then make sure everyone knows what it is.
- Successful marketing usually means personal contact with the potential client.
- Never underestimate the client's intelligence — most you will meet are at least as clever as the average chartered engineer!
- Make sure your contacts are people who either (a) make decisions on consultant selection and/or (b) can give you background information.
- These days, an engineer also has to be a salesman.

3

Invitation

The formal way of getting an invitation

Three-stage consultant selection

The initial marketing exercise is supposed to convince prospective clients that your company is reliable, competent, and generally one of the best in its field. You hope that this will lead to a direct invitation to carry out a new project or, at least, to submit a proposal for a new project. Direct invitations are not unheard of, particularly for the smaller new projects, and for companies who are well-established with a particular client. For the larger projects, clients usually adopt a formal procedure for selecting the successful consultant.

From the client's point of view, some sort of structured selection procedure helps for a number of reasons

- Partly on the grounds of fairness: the first stage is open to as many consultants as want to express an interest in the project, and so gives newcomers to the market a chance to compete.
- Partly because clients want to make a reasoned, objective choice of consultant, rather than an impulsive, subjective choice.
- Partly because clients must appear to be open and impartial, not only to their own internal management, but also to outside bodies (for example, to the banks which provide finance for their loans).
- Partly out of direct self-interest: staff making the choice of consultant do not want to be accused of irrational decisions or even worse, of partiality.
- Partly out of common sense: if a hundred consultants submitted proposals for each project, the client would have to spend an enormous amount of time evaluating them. Staff would be wasting some 99% of their effort,

Table 6. Three-stage consultant selection

Stage	Consultants	Client	Number of consultants involved
Start: client announces details of the new project			
Consultant selection stages			
• Expression of interest	Some consultants advise the client of their interest in carrying out the project	**1st stage selection** The client considers all of the replies and then decides on a long list of companies still in the running for the scheme	start 100+ end 20+
• Pre-qualification	Selected consultants describe their project-related experience and skills	**2nd stage selection** The client eliminates the worst/selects the best. The result produces a shortlist of consultants	start 20+ end 6+
• Proposal	Short-listed consultants describe *how* they would carry out the project, *which staff* they would use, and *how much* it would cost	**3rd stage selection** Submission and evaluation of proposals. The result produces the successful consultant	start 6+ end 1
Client awards the new project			

since only one consultant can win the project anyway (and 99% of the consultants would also be wasting their efforts) The accepted norm is to call for proposals from somewhere between three to six consultants.

Many of these advantages apply to consultants as well — they want clients to seriously evaluate their hard work, and they don't want to put in a great deal of effort if they have very little chance of succeeding. The usual selection process which consultants have to go through has three stages (Table 6). Each stage takes progressively more effort from both the consultant and client, and leaves fewer consultants in the game afterwards.

Start: client announces details of a new project

Many clients — and particularly the large international financing institutions or banks such as the European Bank for Reconstruction and Development — publish news of a new project in an appropriate magazine or newspaper. Many banks have their own, in-house journal. The EBRD, for example, publishes its *Procurement Opportunities* monthly. It has, in addition, a fax service which sends companies details of forthcoming new projects. The EBRD uses the fax service as a way of speeding up its call for expressions of interest, and so if you wait for the *Procurement Opportunities* to arrive before you send one off, you will often be too late. Many project announcements appear in several publications — EBRD-financed schemes also appear in the World bank's regular *Development Business*. Some banks have already begun to advertise their new schemes on their Internet home page. The ADB is one example. This trend will probably increase, since it reduces the time to publish new or updated information about forthcoming schemes, and reduces the cost of printing and distributing paper-based announcements (Table 7).

If you have applied your marketing strategy properly, then you will be aware of new schemes in your area of interest even before the client formally publishes details of them. After all, publications are at best only secondary sources of information. The primary sources are contacts either in the bank which is to finance the scheme, or in the organisation which is promoting it. You will also know more about the schemes than the published information, from your contacts and from your own knowledge of the region and the client.

Not every announcement of a scheme also calls for expressions of interest. This does not mean that sending off such an expression of interest (EOI) now, would be a waste of time — it could mean that your company appears first in the queue. Alternatively, some calls for an expression of interest can be safely ignored; the client is only publishing them as a matter of record, and has already decided which consultant will be awarded the new project. Many of the notices which appear in the European Commission's supplement are like this. Whatever the EU's formal rules of the game suggest, many

Table 7. *Examples of bank publications*

Bank	Publication	Notes
EBRD	*Procurement Opportunities* *Procurement Opportunities* fax service	Monthly Notification of technical cooperation projects
ADB	*ADB Business Opportunities* ADB Internet page	Monthly, covers proposed projects, procurement notices and contract awards
World Bank	*Development Business* World Bank Internet page	

government departments will find reasons to select consultants from their own country. If you come across details of an interesting new project, you should check with your contacts to see whether it is worth submitting an expression of interest or not.

First stage selection: expressions of interest (EOI)

These are also variously known as *letters of interest*, and *registrations of interest*. They are useful to the consultant since they make a quick, formal link between his company and the new project. They help the client, by giving him some idea of which companies are actually interested in the work. Many clients (both banks and sponsoring organisations) have access to databases of consulting companies. These can tell the users which companies could do the work, but cannot tell them which companies want to do it. Some, for example, might have the skills and experience, but not the resources to do it; others may not be interested in working in that particular country.

Generally speaking, you can submit an EOI for any new project which catches your interest. There are two occasions when you should not submit one however.

The first is where your company has little experience, and no full-time specialists in the appropriate disciplines. Like winning a lottery, it doesn't take a great deal of money or effort, and you just might be starting your company on the way to a major new contract. Alternatively, the chances of success are limited, and a weak EOI can lead to serious disadvantages.

- You may upset the client by wasting his time with what will seem a frivolous document (for example, if your company is registered with the client as a transportation specialist, then submitting an EOI for a rural housing project will not be productive).
- You may damage your company's reputation as a serious professional consultant.
- You are wasting your own time, which is as valuable (and limited) as anyone elses'.

The second occasion when you should not submit an EOI is when the client says you shouldn't. For example, some project announcements state that they are open to companies from the client's country only.

Submitting as a joint venture (JV) group If your company doesn't have all the skills which the new project will require, you could still submit an EOI by teaming up with one or more other firms who can provide the missing expertise. Doing so will be easier if you already have good contacts with other firms who are interested in working in the project country; and at this stage, there is no need to exchange formal joint venture agreements or contracts with the other companies. You and your new partner companies should discuss which one should formally submit the EOI — in some cases, for example, it could be helpful if the company from the client's country takes the lead (see above).

What you should say in an EOI Expressions of interest will usually be brief: you are only *expressing* your company's interest in a project, and not trying to describe the history of your firm from the date it was first established. If you do submit an EOI several pages long, complete with brochures and project references, then the client will probably just throw the whole lot away.

Here, as elsewhere in the book, one important rule applies: **answer the question**. If the announcement asks for a one-page EOI you should not send off 20 pages plus two sets of company brochures; but if the announcement asks for some short descriptions of key staff, provide these one-paragraph summaries even if it means the EOI is now three pages long.

Some banks have issued notes on how to apply for an invitation to tender. Where the EOI is not specific, read these notes and call the contact in the bank to check what you should provide. Where you do not have the time to do this, a general guide for EOIs is that they should contain the information suggested in Table 8 and that

Table 8. *Details to include in a letter (expression) of interest*

Client	Project	Your company
Name	Project name	Company name
Address	Project location	Address
Contact name	Project reference	Contact name
Phone/fax numbers	Summary of project	Phone/fax numbers
Date project announced		Registration number with this client
		Statement of interest
		Statement of relevant experience
		Names of any JV partners
		Depending on space available, short details of
		• relevant projects
		• regional experience
		• specialist staff
		• previous clients

Table 9. Time and cost of preparing an EOI

Element	Value*	
	From	To
Time per EOI	1 hour	8 hours
Number per representative per year[†]	800	100
Cost per EOI[‡]	US$50	US$400
Success rate[#§]	1 in 4	1 in 4

[*] These are subjective assessments.
[†] Assumes 200 working days per year, 50% of time spent on other activities.
[‡] Assumes the country representative cost to the company is US$80 000 p.a., including an overheads and social charges multiplier of 2.5.
[#§] Meaning, where the EOI leads to the company proceeding to the second or third stage selection.

- they should be no more than 2–3 pages long
- the cover page should give full basic details such as contact address and telephone numbers
- there should be no more than two additional pages of supporting information.

Time and cost of preparing expressions of interest Once you have decided to submit an EOI, you will have to

- decide what information has to be sent off
- collect it
- type and send off the document.

How much time this will take you depends on how well you and your colleagues have prepared yourselves (Table 9). For example, you should know through your marketing activities what sort of information this particular client expects to see in an EOI. Your company should also have instantly available (and printable) summary details of all its major projects and its current key technical staff. A database would be ideal, but at the very least you should have summary lists of both. Finally, you should already have well-established contacts in (or information about) other companies, for those occasions when you decide to submit a joint EOI.

With this level of efficiency it should be possible to prepare an EOI within an hour — perhaps 30 minutes to collect the information and 30 minutes to type and send it off. Many companies are probably not so well-prepared, and so will need around one day to prepare the document, mostly spent in chasing around for the information and the partner contacts. Even then the result will probably be less than the best quality EOI.

You will spend most of this time collecting the information yourself — particularly when *you* are the country/client representative. You cannot then leave this to a secretary — or anyone else — since *you* are then the person with the contacts, and the person who knows most about the client, the country and the project.

Summary: expressions of interest

- Submit early; never submit late.
- Don't submit EOI for schemes where you really have no experience or skills: (a) you'll look an idiot and (b) you are an idiot.
- Answer the question: submit EOI in the way the client wants them. If you don't know how he wants them, ask.
- Don't send brochures with the EOI. You should already have established your company with the client.
- Keep the EOI short and to the point. Ignore people who tell you to do otherwise.
- Think before you act: it is always possible to send something straight away — sending something *sensible* takes a little more time.
- Information sought for under pressure is the most elusive type of all — collect basic details of projects, key staff, country experience and so on in advance.

Second stage: pre-qualification documents (PQs)

Expressions of interest are just that — they let the client know that a company is interested in carrying out the project. Pre-qualification documents confirm the company's interest, and give the client more details about its relevant experience and capabilities.

Submitting as a joint venture group In asking you to submit a PQ the client will often send you further details of the new project. You should also be using your own contacts and project information to find out more details about it yourself. It is still possible for you to change your mind about whether it is necessary to associate with another company for this project.

What you should say in a PQ The PQ gives you the chance to provide fuller details (Table 10) of your company's relevant past projects — you can even consider including a few photographs. Sending non-relevant information will give the client the impression that either you haven't understood what the new project is about or that you're padding your material because you don't really have any appropriate project experience. If the project deals with the repair of airport runways in a Central European country then

Table 10.   Details to include in a PQ

(a) General

Client	Project	Your company
Name	Project name	Name Company
Address	Project location	Address
Contact	Project reference	Name Contact
Phone/fax numbers	Summary of project	Phone/fax number
Date project announced		Registration number with this client
		Statement of interest
		Names of any JV partners

(b) Specific to the new project

Your company/your JV group

Potential services offered	• business discussion notes (e.g. first notes on organising a project unit) • technical discussion notes (e.g. first notes on problems the project may involve)
Regional experience	• in countries in the same region • in countries at a similar stage of economic development
Project experience	• project size/volume, date • technical summary of relevant projects • client name
Specialist staff	• years of professional experience • key qualifications
Previous clients	• other clients in region of interest • other clients who are of the same type as the new client
Something extra	• interesting possibilities for added value or services

Notes.
You will have noticed that part (a) above is virtually a repetition of the information which an EOI should contain. This suggests that a building block or modular approach to preparing documents could save you time and effort. For a discussion on modules, and on how to structure and present documents, see the section on writing technical proposals.

(a)   a past project repairing runways somewhere in Asia *is* relevant experience
(b)   a past project designing terminal buildings in another central European country is *not*.

You should also send summary profiles of relevant present technical experts. At this stage you don't have to say exactly who would carry out the project, but the people you name should still be capable of carrying out the work involved. In doing all this you should try to give the client as much information as possible, but still within a limited space. If too much information is sent it will receive as much attention as an oversize EOI: it will be thrown straight into the waste paper bin. The PQ should contain a selection of project and key staff, rather than describe everything and everyone who might be remotely relevant to the new project.

Finally, try to say something original and attention-catching. Otherwise you will be one among 20 or so other, capable but just as ordinary engineering consultancies. For example, you could relate your company's skills in rehabilitating airport runways with its experience in using GIS-CAD for facilities management. This could provide the client with a useful if unexpected extra service.

Time and cost of preparing PQs PQs involve the same three steps as an EOI (deciding what information to collect, collecting it and sending it off) — but they require more effort. You should also begin by spending more time in collecting background information on the new project, on the organisation paying for it and on the organisation who will eventually own and use it. The purpose of this is to make sure that the details of your company which you submit in the PQ relate to the details of the new project.

The general time and cost of a PQ once again depends on how well you and your colleagues have prepared yourselves. An additional factor here is the question of working time and calendar time. Preparing the PQ might only need a day of your time, but delivering it can take anything from less than one day to more than two weeks — it depends on how you send it e.g. courier/normal air mail), and where you have to send it to (Table 11).

Finally, again as with an EOI (and for the same reason) you should prepare the PQ largely by yourself. These days engineers should be able to use a computer; if you cannot even type your own material, then you should not be working on international proposals.

Summary: pre-qualification documents

- Collect background information on the project before you prepare a PQ.
- Check what the client wants (as opposed to what his document says he wants).
- Send only relevant information (don't waste the client's time).
- Use your common sense in selecting relevant information (and your contacts with the client).
- Once again, think before you act: you can deliver nonsense today; quality takes a little more time.

Table 11. Time and cost of preparing a PQ

Element	Value*	
	From	To
Time per PQ (working time), made up of	2 days	6 days
• collect background information on project	(1 day)	(2 days)
• select/collect company information	(half-day)	(3 days)
• preparing and sending off PQ	(half-day)	(1 day)
Calendar time per PQ, made up of		
• preparation	2 days	6 days
• delivery	2 days	one week
Number per representative per year[†]	50	30
Cost per EOI[‡]	US$800	US$1350
Success rate[#§]	1 in 5	1 in 5

[*] These are subjective assessments.
[†] Assumes 200 working days per year, 50% of time spent on other activities.
[‡] Assumes the country representative cost to the company is US$80 000 p.a., including an overheads and social charges multiplier of 2.5.
[#§] Meaning, where the EOI leads to the company proceeding to the second or third stage selection.

Third stage: proposals

Clients check through the PQ documents they have received and select a handful of companies who they will invite to submit a proposal. Writing a proposal is important enough to merit a chapter or two of its own; these begin with chapter 5, on 'Preparation'.

Other ways of getting an invitation

Short cuts

If you have carefully applied a sensible marketing strategy, then you will have developed some useful contacts in the target client groups and countries. You will know a lot about them and the way they do business. Just as importantly, they will know you and your company, and the way *both* of you do business. This should mean that the client now sees your company as one which is both competent and reliable. You may then be able to skip one or more steps in the formal way of getting an invitation to submit a proposal, using short cuts such as those detailed below.

Direct invitation to submit an EOI Not a big saving in effort, but it can give you some extra time to look into the background of the project. It also suggests you have more than an even chance of progressing further towards (at least) being asked to send in a proposal. Of course, you may have been annoying the client's representative (rather than developing a good relationship with him). A direct invitation to submit an EOI could be his way of getting rid of you: he will never add your company to any short or long list of preferred consultants.

Direct selection for the long list A successful stage 1: achieving this shows that the client has a serious interest in your company. He is probably also willing to give you a lot of background information on the new scheme.

Direct selection for the short list A successful stage 2: this is the sort of relationship you should hope for with a client; already he is convinced of your company's ability to do the work. He still wants, however, to compare details of the services and costs you are willing to offer, with those of a few other competent companies.

Selection using registration databases or personal knowledge Many banks have developed registers of international consultants. They and other potential clients have access to these registers, and can prepare a long or short list of potentially interesting consultants simply by using the register.

Being asked directly to carry out the project A successful stage 3: you still have to submit some form of proposal — but you are sure to get the project. The proposal will be the means where you and the client can define and agree on the scope and prices for the work your company will be doing.

Suggesting the project yourself It may seem unnecessary to wait for an invitation before writing a proposal — in other words, consultants may want to suggest a new project themselves. This is not necessarily a good idea.

(*a*)   Writing proposals is an exercise which costs a lot of time and money. You don't want to invest all this effort in an exercise whose chances of success you cannot estimate.

(*b*)   Suggesting a worthwhile new project may make a good impression on the client, but that is no reason for him to ask you to carry it out (and no reason for you to write a proposal for it). You may have found a private bank ready to finance the scheme but even that doesn't guarantee your company a new contract.

(*c*)   Suggesting a new scheme can also have direct drawbacks, particularly if you speak to the wrong person. For example, if you spot a gap in Croatia's national railway network the best person to talk to would be someone in the local Ministry of Transport or railway authority — and not with the head of finance of the European Investment Bank (EIB) or EBRD.

Generally, you should not write a proposal until you've been formally asked to.

Why clients sometimes use short cuts in selecting consultants

The formal way of selecting consultants can deliver the company with the most interesting ideas, but it is a very expensive and time-consuming exercise for both the consultant and the client. For smaller projects the effort is not worthwhile. Short cuts save the client time and money.

Time can be particularly important when the client has a crisis on his hands. Perhaps cracks have appeared in the columns of one of his motorway bridges. The client needs expert advice urgently, and will probably call one or two companies directly for quotes, and select on the basis of their replies.

Occasionally a project is particularly specialised, or needs a large helping of local knowledge. Only a few companies could carry it out and the client will already have a good idea who they are. He may choose to begin by preparing the short list of suitable companies.

A client will also use a direct award in order to keep your company's interest alive. He is looking after his own business interests. For example, sometimes a country has a small local consultancy base of its own. A government ministry can support the presence of two or three international companies by occasionally feeding them with contracts. The advantages for the ministry are

- it maintains the presence of a pool of large consultancies with guaranteed local knowledge and experience
- it indirectly encourages joint ventures with local consultants, who can then bid for regional projects as well as in-country ones
- it keeps good relations with large companies for those odd occasions when a crisis develops, and the country urgently needs reliable, expert advice.

Summary: short cuts

- Unknown consultants don't get on to the 'short cuts' trail.
- You will probably still have to write some sort of costed

proposal sooner or later, whatever selection process the client uses.

Consultants' own project selection procedure

If your company's strategy is to chase after every project which seems even remotely interesting, then you don't need a selection procedure of your own (or rather, you are using the 'all-or-nothing' selection procedure — you select all possible projects and succeed in winning none of them). Most companies do have limited resources and prefer to take a more considered approach to deciding which projects they would be interested in applying for. Such companies frequently use a 'structured' approach to project selection. This uses a pre-defined set of questions or a checklist to help you and your colleagues select projects which make business sense.

Two levels of selection

One example of a structured selection procedure would have two levels, each one considering the possible new project in a little more detail.

Level one selection — does it match your company's marketing strategy This is where having a written marketing strategy proves quite useful. If the new project is in a country or in a technical area which the strategy does not include, then you should not spend any more time on it. For example, if your company is interested in selling its highway design skills in South-East Asia, then it should ignore a project for a new power station in Kazakhstan.

There may be times when the scheme does not match your marketing strategy, but still seems interesting — perhaps the Kazakhstan power station project will involve a lot of project management work, an area in which the company is also a leading expert. In this case, (and in cases where the new scheme does match your strategy) the scheme passes through to the next level of selection.

Level two selection — is it worth it Following up projects consumes time and money. The second level selection considers whether the project you've just seen will be worth the effort which you and your company will have to put in to acquire it. Points which you should consider are

- *practical*: for example, has the deadline for submitting an EOI passed; does the project have sound financing

- *business*: do you need to associate with another company; if so, are you still likely to make a reasonable profit from the scheme. Associating with other companies will reduce your profits but not necessarily the costs of preparing a proposal.
- *technical*: does your company have all the specialist staff needed to carry out the project — what will the client think if your own experts are otherwise engaged, and so 95% of the staff you propose are freelancers.

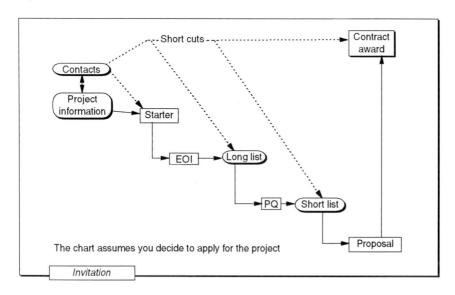

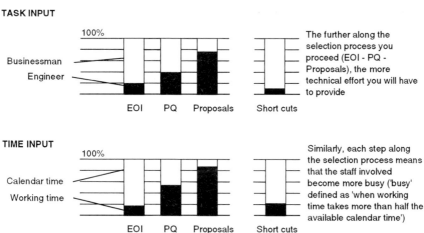

Fig. 5. Formal and informal consultant selection procedures

Making the selection The first level selection will only take a minute provided you have a clearly-defined marketing strategy. The second level will take more time — perhaps a day, allowing you to check with local contacts in the country and find out more about the scheme. Making the decision is a task for the area representative. Whatever the answer, the decision you make isn't final — you may want to review it as you learn more about the scheme.

Risk of turning down invitations If the same client continues to invite you to submit a proposal for a project, and your company continues to decline, then he will begin to think your company is not seriously interested. In such cases there must be something seriously wrong with your marketing strategy — or your company does not have one.

Summary: your own selection procedure

- Use your marketing strategy as a guide, not as a rule book.
- Give priority to following up projects which you have most chance of winning.
- Not having a selection procedure means that you can never be sure whether you overlooked a project, or in fact decided that it was not one which was worth following up.
- If someone does overlook an interesting project, don't complain — find out why and make sure it cannot happen again.

Figure 5 details formal and informal consultant selection procedures.

4

Registrations

General

What is registration?

The story so far: your company has decided to develop new business in international markets, and has developed a marketing strategy. You have put it into practice, and as a result of your own marketing activities, you have heard news of interesting new projects and made useful new contacts. Project information and contacts together have led to an invitation from a client, asking your firm to submit a proposal for one of the schemes. Then you hear that the client operates a system of registering details of consulting companies. Your company is not registered with this particular client, and you wonder whether this means that the client cannot award your company the project.

Of course, it doesn't mean that at all. Registrations are just one way in which some clients obtain details of companies that are interested in working for them. Stored in databases, the registrations can act as an information source for people who want to identify companies with suitable skills and experience for a new scheme. Registrations are not the only information source for the banks which operate them, they do not give preferential status to the companies concerned, and they do not put the client under any obligation to the registered companies. Many clients make this point very emphatically.

Consultants sometimes produce company brochures which include lists showing which banks and other clients they have registered with. The implication is that these banks, by accepting the company's information, have somehow expressed a formal approval of the company. This is not true. Such lists will do nothing to impress the well-informed reader.

If your company believes that sending off the registration documents today means that the client will award your company a new project tomorrow, then they are making another mistake. Registrations as a marketing activity, are overrated. This doesn't mean that they are entirely pointless. They can help you maintain contact with the client; they can focus your attention on your own marketing strategy; and the client may perhaps use the registered information when he prepares long lists or shortlists of suitable companies.

Occasionally, a client actually requires companies to register with him — the United Nations Purchase and Transportation Service (UN/PTS), which is involved in survey and feasibility studies, transportation studies etc, is one example; but this is the exception rather than the rule.

Consultants cannot be sure that the exercise of registration has any real value for either themselves or the client. The process itself can be as complicated as any beaurocratic procedure.

Companies can find that they have to register with the client, then again with one of the client's sub-organisations. They sometimes have to register their details on a computer diskette, sometimes on a paper form — and sometimes on both. Consultants may even have to

- register with the client's main organisation via computer diskette
- register again with the client's main organisation using different paper forms
- register yet again with one of the client's sub-organisations using another paper form.

Registration *is*

- one source of information about consulting firms
- sometimes, a short cut through some of the steps on the path to submitting a proposal
- a method of increasing clients' overhead costs
- inefficient.

Registration *is not*

- the source (through registration databases) from which the client must select companies
- a sign of the client's recognition of the importance or good qualities of your company
- a status symbol for your company
- an assurance that the client will give your company any priority when selecting firms

Table 12. Some comments on registration

Organisation	Registration
UK Overseas Development Administration (ODA)[6]	Registration does not guarantee that a firm will be invited to submit proposals for ODA/British Government funded projects or that the firm has ODA or British Government approval.
UK Overseas Development Administration[7]	*It is essential* that firms show only *genuinely* available skills and experience *otherwise much time and effort will be wasted in processing doubtful data.* (emphasis in the original)
European Bank for Reconstruction and Development[8]	. . . while this (registration) information may be useful to the Bank, it is neither a precondition for being considered for a bank-financed assignment nor is it sufficient to secure such an assignment.
World Bank[9]	Registration . . . does not mean any endorsement by the World Bank of the information on qualifications provided by you (the consulting company)
United Nations Industrial Development Organisation (UNIDO)[10]	Prior registration and expressions of interest are prime elements in the . . . selection of companies . . . to be invited to submit bids/proposals.
United Nations Purchase and Transportion Service (UN/PTS)[11]	Interested parties must complete and submit a technical data questionnaire . . . . The data is incorporated in a roster from which long lists are compiled.
EU Phare's Central Consultancy Register (CCR)	(You should) register only the parent company and declare . . . all your subsidiaries. . . . Should the expertise of one of your subsidiaries be substantially different from the one of the parent company, you may register it separately. If we do not consider this subsidiary's activities to be sufficiently different from the parent company, we will incorporate its experience into the main registration of the parent company.

---

6 ODA *Index of consulting firms — registration application*, page 1, para. 5 (September 1994).

7 ODA *Index of consulting firms — registration application*, page 1, para. 4 (September 1994).

8 EBRD's monthly *Procurement Opportunities*.

9 quoted in a cover letter accompanying the DACON (Data on CONsultants) registration diskette, March 1995.

10 *UNDP United Nations system — general business guide*, page 67 May 1994 edition.

11 UNDP *United Nations System — general business guide*, page 19. May 1994 edition.

- an implied right for your firm to expect work from the client
- essential.

Who and what do you register?

If your firm is only a single company then this question is easy — you can only register as one company. If your firm is part of a group, then the answer depends on what you are trying to achieve, and who you are registering with. The ODA, for example, has to meet the UK government's commitment to the participation of small and medium size enterprises in bidding for public service contracts — which suggests that smaller companies may get preferential treatment. Alternatively the EU Phare's Central Consultancy Register (CCR) states that you should only register the parent company (Table 12).

Registering as a company group The advantages of registering as a group are that you can pool resources for a stronger submission — the group has experience in more countries and sectors, and has more specialist staff, than its individual members taken separately. There is also the potential for linking separate skills into one attractive package. Suppose a group has an associate company based in Prague and a GIS specialist associate in London. It could offer a joint package of GIS skills and experience for the central European PHARE program.

Registering as several companies Where the registration form gives limited space for describing the range of activities your company carries out, then you might need to submit details from separate subsidiaries. For example, the UN's MCVRP (Mandatory Computerized Vendor Re-registration Programme) limits to 25 the number of goods and services the applying firm can claim experience in. And as the CCR suggests, if a particular subsidiary offers unusual or a different range of services, it would be sensible to register it separately.

Registering as individual consultants A number of clients operate registration systems for individuals as well as companies. Consultants can also register individual staff with them as specialists, although this can depend on the client. Some are quite happy with the idea, while others (the EBRD, for example) are concerned that there might be conflicts of interest. They may worry that the individuals will be torn between loyalty to the client and loyalty to their employer.

Who do you register with?

You should be careful about which potential clients you register with, if for no other reason than to save yourself time (and your company's money). For example, if your company's marketing strategy focuses on South-East Asia, then there is little point in registering it with the European Union's Tacis (Technical Assistance to the Commonwealth of Independent States (and Mongolia)) programme. This supports projects in Eastern Europe. Alternatively, if your firm wants to work in Vietnam but doesn't have any regional experience, the material it can submit to the ADB will be very weak. Perhaps it should associate with a local company; you could then send the ADB a joint registration.

International financing institutions are not the only organisations to have registration systems. Most countries have their own cover organisations for consulting firms (the UK's British Consultants Bureau and Germany's VUBI (Verband Unabhängig Beratender Ingenieurfirmen — in English, Association of independent consulting engineering companies) are two examples). Such organisations usually produce handbooks which provide details of their member companies. Clients do actually use the handbooks when selecting consultants for long or short lists, so you should make sure that your company's details are up-to-date, and relevant.

While banks provide funds for a project, they are not necessarily its executing agency. The executing agency — perhaps a national or regional government — can prepare its own selection of consultants, and will sometimes have its own registration system. The initial marketing will show you which of these other clients you should also register with.

What information do you register?

The obvious answer is, 'provide the information which the client asks for in his registration forms'. Life *is* that simple — almost. Most of the registration procedures ask for four main types of information

- *administrative*: company address, telephone and fax numbers, etc.
- *company size*: number of subsidiaries, professional staff, annual fees
- *project references*: projects which illustrate the company's skills and experience
- *key words*: words from pre-defined lists which indicate the company's strengths.

For each type, you should provide the information which the client asks for, which matches your marketing strategy, which is consistent with the information you registered with other banks, and which is correct.

Information matches marketing strategy Select the projects which closely relate to the strategy. If you want to work on highway schemes in South-East Asia, then past schemes which involve railway design in Europe would not be particularly helpful. Some registration forms provide limited space for project references; this will force you to be selective.

Information is consistent Many clients have access to other registration databases besides their own. They may wonder about your company if the data they read varies from database to database. If you tell one client that the power station you worked on in Latvia brought in US$200 000 in fees, then give the other clients the same figure.

Information is correct If the power station in Latvia actually brought you only US$100 000 in fees, then this is the figure you should register. Some clients have begun to ask for contact details of the organisations behind the projects for which you submit references. An exaggerated reference can damage your reputation with all potential clients who have access to the database you registered with, and not just the owner of it.

Key words present a more tricky problem. Many registration databases have them. They serve as sort fields, and help users pick out companies with experience in the right technical area, region, or speciality. What you may understand these words and phrases to mean is not necessarily the same as what the client understands them to mean. It would be helpful if

(*a*)   every database used the same sets of key words and phrases
(*b*)   every database provided definitions of the key words/phrases
— but they don't.

Summary

- Decide who you want to register your company with.
- Check the client's latest registration procedures and policy.
- Make sure you understand the procedures — your understanding of phrases the client uses for sector specialisations may be different to the client's, for example.

- Decide what you want to register (provide information to support your marketing strategy).
- Make sure the information you register is correct.
- Make sure the information you register is consistent.
- Keep your own copy of the information you send away.
- Make sure everyone else in the company knows what you've done (the client's confidence in your company will suffer if two offices submit registration details).
- Remember to update the registration, either when you have an interesting new project reference, or when your current registration has reached the client's stated registration renewal period.
- Banks generally use the *project* sheets to search for potentially suitable companies, rather than the company information sheets.
- Register your best projects, selected to support your marketing strategy. Avoid flooding the bank with information on large numbers of secondary or irrelevant projects.

Examples of registration systems

General

Clients may ask consultants to register on diskette (which they supply), or on paper. In either case, the questions are a mixture of fixed-form and free-form. In *fixed-form* questions the consultant has to tick the boxes which apply to him. For *free-form* questions the consultant has to write a paragraph or two of original text. They cover areas such as the region or countries which the consultant has worked in, and the technical sectors in which he specialises. Usually each country, sector and technical area has a specific code number. These days most clients use computer databases to store registration details. The fixed-form questions make it easier for them to carry out structured sorts through their database.

Besides filling in the diskette or paper-forms, companies often have to provide a range of additional information, for example as evidence in support of the experience they claim to have. Table 13 shows some of the information which the UK's Overseas Development Administration asks for.

It is interesting to compare what procedures different clients use in allowing companies to register with them. The following notes cover (in no particular order): the ODA, the EBRD, the EU (Phare), the European Commission, the World Bank, the United Nations Development Programme (UNDP) and the EIB.

Table 13. *Some details of the ODA registration form*

Information requested	Notes	Example
General	Company address etc. Full-time, permanent members of staff who are based in the UK	Free-form
Company experience		Fixed form tables
Countries	Countries in which the firm has worked in the last five years. The forms list over 160 countries, each of which has a reference code	Afghanistan (code 137)
Sector of experience	Technical sector in which the firm is claiming experience. The forms list ten sectors	Engineering sector
Sub-sector	The sectors are split into around 50 sub-sectors, each with a reference code	Engineering sector: road (80100) rail (80200)
Technical discipline	The sub-sectors are further divided into a series of almost 600 technical disciplines, again each with a code number	road sub-sector: road safety (80106) urban roads (80111)
Type of service	Consultants can claim experience in providing one or more of six types of service carried out on projects in the technical disciplines they highlight	D = design R = research
Additional information		
Project references	One for each main field or specialism claimed	Details include capital value and fee class
CVs	Professional permanent staff	
Statements of capability	E.g. references from previous clients	
Other	Confirmation of overseas work experience	

Overseas Development Administration[12]

The ODA is the British government department responsible for aid to developing countries and to Eastern Europe and the Soviet Union. It maintains a consultancy index which holds details of firms/ organisations who are interested in working on ODA aid-funded projects.

---

12 These notes include quotes from the ODA papers listed in the appendices.

Registration method Consultants complete paper forms, which have to be accompanied by a range of other information. Registrations are for a two-year period, but companies can send in new information when they wish[13]

Valid project references The ODA is quite clear about what projects a consulting company should submit details of: they must have been carried out by the firm as *prime consultant* and during *the last, five, years.*[14]

Information requested There are two sets of information which the consultant has to provide. The paper registration forms make up one set. He has to fill in check lists to indicate which countries and sectors his company has experience in, and to show what type of services he carried out. The second set covers additional and confirmatory detail. For example, he has to describe at least one project in each main field or specialisation in which he claims to have experience. The extra information includes[15]

- project details for each specialisation
- statements of capability (e.g. references from previous clients)
- CVs of professional permanent staff
- confirmation that the company has some experience of working overseas.

Comments The statement under *valid project references* above suggests that 'shell' or 'brass plate' firms — companies with a small administration department and which use mostly part-time and freelance staff — would not have much success with the ODA. It also implies that the Administration does not believe that the age of a company has any bearing on the skills it may have today (e.g. project references should not be more than five years old). Alternatively, the ODA accepts as valid firms even those with only two members of full-time professional staff.[16]

---

13 ODA *Index of consulting firms — registration application*, page 1, para. 3 (September 1994).

14 ODA *Index of consulting firms — registration application*, page 3, item 16 (September 1994).

15 ODA *Index of consulting firms — registration application*, page 1, para. 6 (September 1994).

16 ODA *British overseas aid — arrangements for overseas consultancy services*, annex 2 March 1994.

European Bank for Reconstruction and Development

> The purpose of the EBRD is to foster the transition towards market-oriented economies and to promote private entre-preneurial initiative in the countries of Central and Eastern Europe, including the former Soviet Union . . . One of the primary conditions for meeting this purpose is to build the necessary institutional infrastructure . . . Particular attention is given to financial restructuring, telecommunications, transport, energy and the environment.[17]

Registration method The EBRD at one time introduced a diskette-based registration system for consultants. Recent advice from their Consultants Contracts Unit (CCU) is that the registration system is to be withdrawn. The CCU point out that they have access to the World Bank's DACON system and to a number of other commercial databases. They also pointed out that a reasonable amount of personal contact with representatives of consulting companies could increase their awareness of the companies' potentials.

Some subsidiary databases within the EBRD organisation may continue, such as one for registering details of consulting firms who specialise in the environmental sector.

United Nations

The UN is a complex system of organisations and specialised agencies. Many of them are involved in international development and use the services of consultants. The specialised agencies have their own legislative and executive bodies, their own secretariats and their own budgets. The UN also has regional commissions. In recent years the work of these commissions has been expanded, and they are now increasingly involved in carrying out development projects.[18] Finally, there are the regional banks: not formally part of the UN system, they nevertheless work closely with UN agencies and act as Executing Agencies for development projects financed by the UNDP. Table 14 gives some examples of these different bodies.

Registration method Registration with UN organisations is almost as complex as is the UN system of organisations itself. Somewhere

---

17   EBRD pamphlet *Information for consultants*, March 1993.

18   These notes are based on the *United Nations system — general business guide*, prepared by the UNDP, 16th edition, July 1996.

Table 14. Some examples of UN-related institutions

Type	Name	Abbreviation
Organisation	United Nations Development Programme	UNDP
	United Nations Secretariat	UNS
Specialised	World Bank Group	WB
agency	International Monetary Fund	IMF
	United Nations Industrial Development Organisation	UNIDO
Regional	UN Economic Commission for Europe	UNECE
commission	UN Economic and Social Commission for Western Asia	UN ESCWA
Regional banks	Asian Development Bank	ADB
	African Development Bank	AFDB
	Inter-American Development Bank	IADB
	Caribbean Development Bank	CDB

near the top of the structure seems to be the UN Secretariat. Two departments within the secretariat arrange for the registration programme. The departments are the purchase and transportation service and the department for development support and management services. Or, to use the UN's own words[19]

> ... three organisational units of the Secretariat are involved in procurement, (i) Procurement and Transportation Division (UN/PTD), Department of Administration and Management; (ii) Field Administration and Logistics Division (UN/FALD), Department of Peace-Keeping Operations; and (iii) Contracts and Procurement Service (CPS), Department of Development Support and Management Services (DDSMS). The Secretariat also maintains an office in Geneva, United Nations Office at Geneva (UNOG), which has its own procurement office, Purchase and Transportation Section.

The two departments are responsible for re-registering consultants and other suppliers of goods and services, through the UN Mandatory Computerised Vendor Re-Registration Programme (MCVRP). However, other UN organisations have and maintain their own registration systems. For example.

- UNIDO maintains computerized rosters of Industrial/ Consulting Firms/Organisations and Vendors of Equip-

---

19 UNDP *United Nations system — general business guide*, page 16, July 1996 edition.

ment. Registration in the appropriate roster requires the completion of a questionaire obtainable from UNIDO[20]

- UNOPS [United Nations Office for Project Services] procures goods and services mostly *through limited solicitation of competitive bids proposals*, i.e. by UNOPS invitation to shortlisted entries. Accordingly, UNOPS maintains roster for the identification of such potential suppliers of goods and services.[21]

— and of course the World Bank has its own DACON system of consultants registration.

Valid project references Project references should be for work undertaken in the last ten years. Consultants should give at least one reference for each field of activity in which they claim expertise. No more than one reference per activity should be for work carried out in the home country. The MCVRP accepts registration from company groups and from branch offices and subsidiaries.[22]

Information requested The MCVRP method for consultants requires them to complete a diskette registration, certify a print-out copy of the data, and complete a different, paper registration form (form TCD. 176). As its title says, this registration system is mandatory. In addition the diskette form asks for a copy of the firm's most recent audited financial report.

Comments There is duplication between the DACON system, the MCVRP diskette, the paper form TCD. 176, and the forms and registration methods which various other departments of the UN use. The UN's registration system seems very complicated.

EU Phare (The Phare and Tacis Central Consultancy Register)

The Phare Programme is a European Union initiative which provides grant finance to support its partner countries in Central and Eastern Europe. Key areas for Phare funding include transport and telecommunications infrastructure, and environment and nuclear safety. For

---

20 UNDP *United Nations System — general business guide*, page 66, July 1996 edition.

21 UNDP *United Nations System — general business guide*, page 26, July 1996 edition.

22 United Nations technical data questionnaire TCD. 176, 1995.

countries which have signed Europe Agreements, Phare funding also concerns the development of infrastructure, especially in the border regions.[23]

Registration method The EU Phare and Tacis programmes have a Central Consultancy Register. Consultants complete paper forms, which have to be returned with a range of other information. The most important of these is a *presentation dossier* which should describe the national/international experience of their company, and contain summary descriptions of sample projects. The description should have at least one project description for each claimed area of expertise. The description should preferably be in the format which the CCR suggests, and include details such as the name of the international organisation for which they carried out the scheme, and the name of a contact within the organisation. The CCR automatically sends firms a yearly update reminder.

Valid project references The CCR does not appear to define any specific restrictions, on the age or otherwise, of the project references you decide to give.

Information requested Companies have to return the paper CCR registration forms, plus

- a copy of the statutes or articles of association/partnership of your organisation
- the presentation dossier, (maximum 25 pages) including a brief general presentation of the company, and summary project descriptions with client names and contacts.

Comments The CCR notes that the register is

> used as an important source of information in drawing up of short lists within the tender procedure, (but that) being registered . . . does not guarantee inclusion in a short list.[24]

There is a growing tendency for clients to ask for *statements of capability* from organisations whom consulting firms have worked for (e.g. ODA), or at least contact names within such organisations, who they can later telephone for a reference. An impartial observer might ask whether this is because some consulting firms have not

---

23 *EU Phare programme and contract information 1995*, page 4.

24 EU Phare/Tacis Central Consultancy Register, introductory notes to the registration forms.

been altogether truthful in the past, so far as their claimed work experience is concerned.

European Commission

The European Commission has its own, paper-based registration system, which very largely is identical with the DACON system. The commission is considering setting up a working party to investigate whether they should convert to a diskette-based system, or even one which is accessed through the Internet.

Comments The commission's working party might also review whether the benefits of running a parallel DACON system (albeit with some limited changes), outweigh the costs to all parties concerned.

DACON (Data on CONsultants)

The World Bank provides financial and technical assistance to developing countries to stimulate economic development. It consists of four legally and financially distinct institutions[25]

- the IBRD (International Bank for Reconstruction and Development) – (loans)
- the IDA (International Development Association) – (credits)
- the IFC (International Financial Corporation)
- the MIGA (Multilateral Investment Guarantee Agency).

The last two work specifically with the private sector. The World Bank's DACON registration system is available to or used directly by a number of other banks and financing institutions.

Registration method[26] The World Bank issues consulting firms and individual specialists with a diskette-based registration form, and advises that the registrations should be updated at least every three years. They will remove data which has *not* been updated after this time interval. Providing inaccurate information may result in the elimination of the firm from the database. Users can install the registration program on their computer's hard disk, and download the completed form on to a fresh diskette for forwarding on to the

---

25 UNDP *United Nations system — general business guide,* page 55 May 1994 edition.

26 Based on World Bank's *DACON registration guide* and cover letter, March 1995.

Bank. The Bank will in turn (and for a small payment) issue companies with a hard copy of their registration as it appears in the DACON database. The Bank stores individual consultant's data in a separate database, CHRIS (Computerised Human Resource Information System).[27]

Valid project references Companies who want to register must have at least five full-time professional staff. The projects which companies refer to should be ones which they carried out in the last five years, have involved more than two staff members, and have cost more than

(a)   US$100 000, or
(b)   10% of the total annual fees — whichever is the lowest.

Information requested Companies can provide basic information about themselves, such as contact addresses, gross fees earned as prime and as associate consultant, branch offices outside own country, and so on. They can also include up to 150 valid project references, and may choose to send the Bank additional information such as brochures and annual reports.

Comments The Word Bank registration diskette is easy to use, if based on old fashioned (i.e. not Windows-based, not mouse-driven) software.

European Investment Bank

Registration method The EIB does not have an official registration procedure. They (or the project's promoters) can prepare short lists or select individual consultants on the basis of the consultant's reputation, by recommendation, from the Bank's network of professional contacts, and/or by referring to a particular country's register of consultancies (the handbook of the UK's Association of Consulting Engineers might be an example).

Comments The EIB and its promoters can also use registers of consultants/experts compiled by institutions such as the World Bank and the European Commission.

For further information see Table 15.

---

27 World Bank's *DACON registration guide* and cover letter, March 1995.

Table 15. Summary notes on registration methods applied by some banks*

General area	Paper form	Diskette form	Ease of use	DACON access	Summary
ODA	Good	–	Fair	?	Asks for too much additional information
EBRD	–	–	–	–	System presently under review
UN	Fair	Fair	Fair	Yes	Too many sub-organisations with too many separate registration systems. They should all be closed down and replaced by (perhaps) an improved DACON.
EU Phare	Fair	–	Fair	?	Is it necessary to provide client names and addresses at this stage of the consultant selection process?
EC	–	–	Good	Duplicate	The benefits of using the European Commission modified version of the DACON forms may be less than the costs
World Bank	–	Good	Good	Most definitely	Quite an easy registration method, with an exhaustive set of key words, for which the Bank even provides a lexicon (through the UN's Inter-Agency Procurement Services Office) in Denmark
EIB	–	–	High	Yes?	The EIB may question the value of multiple registration databases

* Further summaries are shown in Table 16 and Fig. 6.

Advantages and disadvantages of the registration system

Consulting companies can invest considerable staff time and resources in registering with the various international financing institutions. They usually do so because it seems to make business sense, and rarely because they *know* it makes sense. Their staff should ask themselves the following questions before rushing into a period of intensive form-filling.

Do registrations bring contacts? Consultants register by completing paper or computer-based forms. If you want to make contact with a piece of paper, then registering is an excellent way of doing so. Alternatively, if you believe that it is more important to make contact with people, then registrations are no great help. At most you can use them as an excuse to telephone or visit people in the bank you are interested in

- Registrations are not a prime source of contacts.

Do registrations bring project information? Companies can subscribe to publications such as the ADB's *'Business Opportunities'* simply by paying the subscription fee. They do not need to have registered with the Bank. Consultants can also call officers in the Bank for more detailed project information, again without being registered. There is also the point that banks are neither the only nor the *primary* source of project information.

- Registrations do not necessarily bring project information.

Do registrations bring status? Some companies include details of their registrations in their general promotional papers. They believe that linking their name with those of the European Bank for Reconstruction and Development, the World Bank, the African Development Bank and so on, will impress the reader. Such a list certainly does not impress the informed reader; and the uninformed reader is unlikely to be someone with a lot of money to spend on hiring the company's services. Many of the banks strongly object to the practice, and point out that the fact of a company being registered with them does not imply that they approve or value the company in any way.

- Registrations do not bring status.

The pseudo-success rate of registering with many banks There is an insidious danger in the excitement of successfully completing a registration form. The act of registration can become an aim in itself, rather than simply a means to an end — acquiring a new project. Company management and international staff can wind up in a closed loop, where the whole act of international marketing reduces to one of maintaining and extending a list of registrations.

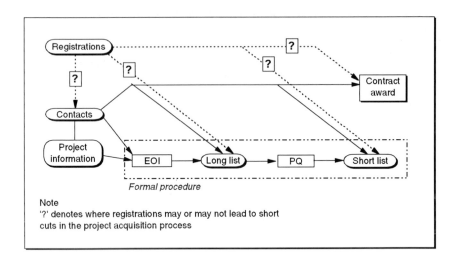

Note
'?' denotes where registrations may or may not lead to short cuts in the project acquisition process

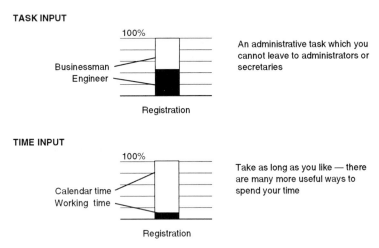

Fig. 6. Value of registrations

Summary: registrations The registration system does have some advantages for consultants. Simply being registered can mean selection for a project long or shortlist, and the process can help the marketing team develop an understanding of what the bank is interested in. More generally, however, it is an excessive consumer of both the banks' and the consultants' resources. The fault lies partly with the banks: they do not have a common registration system, some of the systems they use are not user-friendly, and the systems usually do not allow scope for registering new technology products such as GIS-based highway management methods. The next time someone

Table 16. Advantages and disadvantages of the registration system

Banks	
Advantages	• Gives basic data on consultants, easily accessible • Can help when they have to select long and short lists with special characteristics, e.g. a wide country spread • Can serve as a memory refresher
Disadvantages	• Registration databases are never up-to-date (renewal periods vary from one to three years) • Fixed key-word lists cannot highlight new products (such as GIS-T, pavement management) • Costs both consultants and clients time and money to operate/use • Data supplied is not necessarily true or reliable

Consultants	
Advantages	• Can be a secondary tool in jumping some of the steps in the formal selection process • Can be a requirement for long or shortlisting
Disadvantages	• Registration databases are never up-to-date (renewal periods vary from one to three years) • Fixed key-word lists cannot highlight new products (such as GIS-T, pavement management) • Costs both consultants and clients time and money to operate/use • Doesn't bring companies any closer to the clients • Some of the questions on the registration forms can be misleading. Apparently banks use the project sheets for a key category search/match procedure, rather than the stated company specialisations

asks you to register your company with a bank, remember that registration may lead to your firm

- being added to the registration database – and it may not
- being directly selected for a long or short list – and it may not
- being directly awarded a contract – and it may not.

Summary

- Only register with the banks who are active in areas or subjects which match your marketing strategy.
- Have your business representative complete the registration details.
- Register the company details and experience which best support your marketing strategy.
- Make sure the information you register is correct.

- Make sure the details you register with one bank give the same information as those which you register with the other banks.
- Preferably, only register details of those projects which left your client a satisfied customer.

5

Proposals' preparation

Overview of preparing a proposal

Suppose that a client has now asked your company to submit a proposal for a new project. If the first thing you do is organise a small office party, well and good. You certainly have something to celebrate: from an initial one in a hundred chance of winning the contract you now have a one in six chance of winning it.[28,29] What you certainly should *not* do is to go away and start writing the proposal. Like every other engineering task, the first step is **good preparation**. You need answers to the basic who, what, when, how questions, such as

- *who* is going to write the proposal (is one person alone to write the engineering text, type and proofread it, prepare the graphics and charts)
- *what* are you going to write about (for example, should the text emphasise project management techniques, technology transfer, or just specialist engineering experience)
- *when* do you have to finish the document (when do you have to complete the technical proposal, when does the client want the financial proposal)
- *how* are you going to write the proposal (from one office

---

28 For example the Fédération International Des Ingénieurs-Conseils (FIDIC) *Tendering procedure for obtaining and evaluating tenders for civil engineering contracts*, 1994, page 7, 'for most projects, the number on such a list (of selected tenderers) should be not more than 7'.

29 Also, the World Bank's *Guide to international business opportunities in projects funded by the World Bank*, page 22, 'the short list, not containing more than six firms . . .'

or from more than one; using project management software or simply text and spreadsheet software).

Three phases and eight stages

It is possible to break the work of preparing to write a proposal into a number of stages (Table 17). This should make life easier, using the principle that it is simpler to solve many small problems one at a time, than it is to solve one big problem all at once. Preparation covers four main stages; after these have been completed, work can begin on writing and eventually submitting the proposal documents.

Preliminary review

This involves

- terms of reference
- task definition
- background research
- introduction to evaluation systems
- project staff
- project partners
- decisions.

Table 17. Three phases and eight stages in writing a proposal

Stage	Purpose
Proposals preparation phase	
1. Preliminary review	Decide who to involve in the end project; first steps cover activities such as
	• terms of reference • evaluation systems
	• task definition • project staff
	• background research • project partners
2. Start-up	Decide who, when and how to prepare the proposal, and set up
	• proposals team • proposals office
	• proposals programme • proposals budget
3. Brainstorming	Discuss how to carry out the end project
4. Site visit	Collect detailed information about the project
Core phase	
5. Technical proposal	Prepare draft technical proposal
6. Financial proposal	Prepare draft financial proposal
7. Comparison	Technical and style QA (Quality Assurance) checks
Submission	
8. Delivery	Send off the copies

One of the main sections of the technical proposal will describe how the consultant proposes to carry out the work required of him. This means that he first has to have some idea of what the work actually is. For example, the scheme may involve the supervision of a rural road construction contract, and so the consultant could decide that he needs experienced supervision engineers. However the client may be looking for consultants with project management experience, intending to provide the direct supervision staff himself. Or perhaps most of the new route will follow the alignment of an existing one, and the client wants a pavement management expert to reuse as much of the old road pavement as possible. Again, if the rural road runs close to a number of villages, the consultant will have to provide traffic safety experts to help with the design and location of new accesses.

The best way to succeed in any examination is to read (and understand) the questions. The same principle applies with proposals, and the place to look for the question is in the Terms of Reference.

Terms of reference (TOR)

When a project executing agency invites consultants to submit technical and financial proposals for a project, it does this by sending out a letter of invitation (LOI), accompanied by Terms of Reference. The Terms of Reference (TOR) are documents which provide the consultants with some information on the project, and on what the client expects from him. They should at least contain [30]

- the statement of work to be carried out
- supporting documentation and data relating to the work
- submission or closing date for the proposal documents
- basis of evaluating the submitted proposals
- a statement of information which consultants should include in their proposal.

Generally speaking the TOR contain all this information, and more (Table 18). It is possible to sort it under four broad headings:

Administrative notes These tell the reader when and where to send his proposals, how many copies the client wants, and what language

---

30 FIDIC *Guidelines on quality-based selection of consulting engineers* page 5, 1991.

he wants them in. The client often asks for consultants to confirm that they will submit a proposal, and this should be one of the first things he should do — provided he does decide to submit a proposal.

Background notes These describe details of the client's objectives — the purpose and benefits which the completed project is meant to provide. They also describe the size and scope of the project, and often give some explanation of its historical development and regional significance.

Preparation notes These set out how the client expects the technical and financial proposals to be submitted. Consultants may have other ideas (and the other ideas may be better) but ignoring the clients' stated requirement will only lose points, not win them. Clients often list the formal tasks which the consultant should provide, and explain how they will evaluate the submitted proposals. Both these are indications to the proposal writer. He should not take the client's stated task list as complete or correct, but it is a useful starting point.

Table 18. Information typically supplied with the Terms of Reference

Administrative notes	Letter of invitation (LOI)
	List of short-listed consultants
	Submission details (addresses, number of copies, deadlines)
	Negotiations methods
	Draft contract for consultants' services
	General regulations and other legal statements
	Details of languages (for the proposal; for the services)
Background notes	Project objectives and scope of the services required
	Background information on the project
	List of background material and sources
	Location plan
Preparation notes	Structure and contents of the technical proposal
	Structure and contents of the financial proposal
	Tasks which the consultant has to undertake
	Evaluation methods and weighting
	Indication of required staff (specialisation and man — month inputs)
	Other specific requirements (e.g. requirement for a local partner)
Client-specified forms	Biodata
	Project references
	Financial information
	Other

The client's proposed evaluation method will indicate what services or areas he considers particularly important, and here the writer should pay particular attention — there is no sense in concentrating on writing a very long and detailed chapter on the methodology your company would use if chosen to carry out the project, if the client is mainly interested in the key staff which you propose.

Client-specified forms Most clients ask for detailed project references from the company, and detailed CVs of the staff it selects for the project. The details they ask for are generally the same, but each will ask for the information to be presented in a different way. This can cause consultants some considerable inconvenience. However, working on the principle that 'the customer is always right', consultants presently have to use the forms which the client specifies.

Task definition

Reading the TOR will give you some indication of what the client expects from the successful consultant. But the TOR rarely give a clear and specific definition of tasks involved, and they *never* give a complete list of them. One reason for these incomplete task definitions is that the client may know what he wants, but he is not so sure about how best to obtain it (the uncertainty is one reason why he wants to hire a consultant). A second reason is that the client wrote the TOR some weeks before the consultants received them. During this time changing circumstances may have led to changes in his priorities. The third, and main reason, why the TOR do not give a full task list has to do with the meaning of *tasks*; and here consultancy services usually involve four different explanations and types of task:

- *client requested*: tasks which the client specifies in the TOR
- *consultant proposed*: tasks which the consultant believes would sensibly benefit the project
- *consultant suggested*: tasks which the consultant believes would help the client, but are not essential to the project (and which the consultant would carry out, but perhaps for additional fees)
- *client desired*: tasks which the client has not put in writing.

The TOR will contain only the first type of task. Clients cannot think of the next two types of task (see above, the first reason) and some of those which they do have in mind are not the sort they would want to write down. For example:

- *client-requested tasks*

  o encourage technology transfer by training technical staff in the latest engineering techniques
  o review and update the engineering designs
  o review the environmental impact of the scheme

- *client-desired tasks*

  o provide a free trip to Europe for a number of selected senior management staff
  o provide the client with a modern computer plus associated hardware and software
  o don't bother with the environmental impact of the scheme.

Purpose of task definition In any activity, the first step is to define what exactly has to be done. Only then is it possible to decide in what order it has to be done, what resources are needed, and so on. That is the purpose of task definition. In writing the proposal you will need to state the type and man – months of the personnel who will carry it out, and estimate the associated salary, travel and other costs which the work will involve. You also have to decide whether your company has the expertise to provide all the services required, or whether you need to look for a partner. This principle, of progressing from

(*a*)   task definition through
(*b*)   identifying the type of resources each task will need, to
(*c*)   estimating the amount of resources each task will need, to
(*d*)   providing a balanced programme of tasks at a minimum in resource consumption

is the basis of all sound project management, from preparing to bake a cake to preparing to write a proposal.

Preparing a task list Prepare the first draft of the task list by reading the TOR and writing down what the successful consultant will have to do. Write it as a list, and keep the list in a sensible order (don't start with the final report and finish with a task covering initial data surveys). If you think of any other possible tasks (see the different types of task described above), add them to the list. Finally, keep the list to one page if possible.

Background research

The TOR will give you some idea of what the project will involve, but they will not tell you everything that you should know about the project (there isn't enough room), nor about the best way to carry it out. You should follow up receipt of the TOR with some problem-specific background research — research into climate, for example. Road construction in tropical regions gives rise to a different set of technical problems to road construction in desert regions. In the former, construction may have to close down during the monsoon season, and the scheme will probably involve extensive culvert and minor bridge works. In arid regions the consultant may have to design special barriers or fencing to block wind-blown sand building up on the new carriageway.

In carrying out background research you should take time to consider both engineering and non-engineering fields as, for example

- *climate*: (as in the above example)
- *history*: it is worth knowing something about the project region's history; more directly, it is worthwhile finding out something about the history of the project. For example, if the scheme involves maintainance of an existing road, you should find out when it was built (age of the original material) what design standards the original design engineers worked to, who designed it, etc.
- *location*: is the scheme in a rural or urban area; how good are the local transport and communications connections
- *society*: which days of the week form the local weekend; what are the local business hours; does society accept women professionals; what are the conventional rules of behaviour; should you be looking for labour-intensive or labour-saving techniques
- *politics*: to identify administrative boundaries; at another level, to understand the potential difficulties which can arise from cross-border studies
- *religion*: one company working in a country in the Arabian Gulf included in their project inception report a plan showing the location of mosques and other public buildings. To indicate the mosques they used a symbol similar to the Star of David. The company's clients found that to be particularly insensitive, and took the company off the project. Islamic states have one month of the year where working hours and work progress can be substantially different from the norm.

To emphasise the importance of these points it is worth noting that the ADB (for example) has said that

> Familiarity with the language and customs of the country in which the work is to be performed should be given due consideration (in the evaluation).[31]

Local knowledge Collecting background information and incorporating it into the proposal will make the difference between a good but unsuccessful submission and a good, *successful* submission. It shows the client that you have local knowledge, and that you have taken care to find out about his particular problems — and, even if the problems are not particularly new to him, they may be new to your company. Local knowledge will allow you to describe your approach using examples which the client will be familiar with: explaining minor bridge maintenance to a Vietnamese government official using examples from your knowledge of Venezuela will be less effective than using examples gleaned from a knowledge of Vietnam.

Sources of background information Consultants have a number of sources for their background information. The quickest source would be other proposals which they wrote earlier for projects in the same region of interest. A local office or partner would be able to provide a great deal of background information, not least in suggesting where the main problems will lie (and if your company doesn't have any local office, partner or contact, perhaps it shouldn't be trying to win a project in the area in the first place). Travel guides can explain the basics of the region to someone who has never visited it, while other fact books and sources such as the Economist Intelligence Unit's (EIU) cost-of-living surveys[32] give a lot of useful statistical data. Of course, the most productive (in theory) but also the slowest and most expensive source of background information, is the site visit. Sources of background information include

- other proposals (why re-invent the wheel)
- local office, local partner or other local contacts
- contacts in the financing institution
- travel guides and other country-specific fact books

---

31 ADB *'Guidelines on the use of consultants by the ADB and its borrowers'*, 1996 reprint, para 6.10.(a).

32 EIU, 15 Regent St. London SW1Y 4LR/fax: (004–171) 491–2107.

- local design standards
- other local, project-related documents (e.g. feasibility studies, traffic survey reports)
- the site visit.

Introduction to evaluation systems

Most clients, and certainly most of the banks, include in their TOR some information about the way they will evaluate the proposals. They need a formal system of evaluation to give some structure to the reviewer's assessment, and to avoid a purely subjective recommendation (see discussion in chapter 4). Consultants are also interested in the details of the evaluation system, since it can show where the client's priorities lie. If, for example, the client puts 60% of the evaluation points on the quality of the proposed staff, then the consultant would be unwise to concentrate his efforts in selecting the most appropriate computer hardware and software for the project.

The TOR do not contain all the details of the client's evaluation system. The writer has to look for three different types of guideline; the formal evaluation system, administrative notes, and an unwritten evaluation system.

- *Formal evaluation system*: where for example the TOR explain that the reviewers should give a maximum of 60% to the proposed key staff, that a third of these points depend on the length of an individual's relative professional experience, and so on (Tables 19 and 20).
- *Administrative notes*: specific statements in the TOR such as 'consultants should not include company brochures in their proposal submissions', or 'sections 3 through 6 of the proposal should not contain more than 50 pages', or 'each CV must be signed', or 'the proposals should reach this office no later than the 9th September'. Ignoring such statements — particularly the last one — can lose you up to 100% of the evaluation points with no effort at all.
- *Unwritten evaluation system*: this has more to do with business than with engineering skills. Clients may put a political bias on their selection (for example, not selecting an American company because of current disagreement between their country's central government and that of the USA, or because US companies are already heavily involved in other consultancy work in their country). Other unwritten factors that can influence the choice of the successful proposal include

    ○   subjective appeal — the document is attractively presented, easy to read, and not too long

    ○   personal preference — the reviewer studied in the consultant's home country

    ○   bribery — someone in the consultant's team has given the reviewer a special incentive.

Some evaluation systems include a consideration of the price of the consultants services — the sum of the estimates covered in his financial proposal. The final ranking then becomes a combination of values for the technical and financial proposals. FIDIC recommends that the weighted value of the price should be 10% as a maximum.[33]

Of the basis which clients actually use to select a winning proposal, perhaps, 60% of their decision relates to the technical evaluation, 20% to the reviewer's subjective opinion and 20% to the client's business politics. Whatever the weighting, you will find that it pays to begin with an understanding of the client's evaluation system.

Table 19. Examples of formal evaluation systems* for technical proposals

Evaluation area	Max. points awarded	Evaluation sub-area	Max. points awarded
Company experience	15	Technical sector	10
		Regional experience	2
		Other (e.g. backstopping)	3
Approach and methodology	25	Understanding of tasks	5
		Task/resource allocation	5
		Work plan	5
		Innovation	3
		Man – month needs	2
		Proposal presentation	2
		Other	3
Key personnel	60	General qualifications	10
		Technical adequacy	35
		Language skills	5
		Regional experience	5
		Training ability	5
Total	100		

* The above is based on a number of TOR documents, and is meant only as an indication – read the TOR for the project for which you are writing the proposal.

33 FIDIC, *Selection by ability — guidelines on quality-based selection of consulting engineers*, page 7, 1991.

Table 20.   Example of evaluation points* for key personnel

General qualifications	**10**	Education and training	3
		Length of relevant experience	3
		Length with firm	2
		Type of position held	2
Technical adequacy	**35**	Coordination and liaison	10
		Administration	5
		Specific technical experience	20
Language skills	**5**	English	4
		Local language	1
Regional experience	**5**	Regional experience	5
Training ability	**5**	Formal training courses	2
		On-the-job training	2
		Developing country training	1
Total	**60**		

* The above is also meant only as an indication — collect the appropriate background information for the project you are actually involved in.

Project staff

The TOR will often include an indication of the key personnel the client expects. You will be able to compare this with your own estimate of the experts needed to carry out the work described in your first task list. If your company cannot provide the full range of experts from its own resources, you may need to associate with another firm.

Your company also has to decide who is to lead the work on the proposal itself. Like any other project, one person has to be in charge. The best choice would be a technical expert with some regional knowledge, rather than a regional representative with some technical knowledge. In either case, if your company nominates you to be the proposal leader, you should make sure that everyone involved is made aware of it. There is nothing worse than working on a project where two people are making the decisions.

Project partners

There are a number of reasons for looking for a partner company. One is that a partner can provide expertise in those areas of the project where your own company is weak — perhaps because it does not have the specialist staff, or perhaps because its in-country experience is weak. A second reason is that the TOR may require you to team up with a local company. The client's aim in such cases is partly to encourage technology transfer, and sometimes to keep the costs of the project low (this is another reason why you may choose to work with a local consultant).

Selecting partner companies depends on whether the potential partner has something technically worthwhile to offer — but usually you can find more than one firm to choose from. The choice also has to consider business questions such as the potential for long-term cooperation on other national and international projects. You will have to decide on the relative importance of the technical and business parts of these decisions on a case-by-case basis.

Your company may have developed links with potential partners when it set out its marketing strategy, or when it prepared the EOI or PQ document. If not, and assuming you are indeed the proposal leader, you should begin initial discussions with potential partner companies now. Bear in mind that the relationship with these partners may develop into a full, joint venture association, they may become sub-consultants or simply informal suppliers of one or two specialist staff.

Decisions

Your company is still not yet committed to submitting a proposal. No doubt it can *technically* complete the project to everyone's satisfaction; but after completing the preliminary review the company management may wonder whether there is any financial or other profit to be made from it. Writing a proposal is not always worth the effort and risk. You should take the time to review again *business* considerations such as

- comparing the cost of preparing and writing the proposal documents, against the 1 in 6 chance that your company will win the project
- possibly upsetting the client and financing agency by withdrawing now (after your company made so much effort to be short-listed)
- comparing your company's likely costs against the profits which may be made from its share of the services and staff to be supplied
- seeing the project as a loss-leader to opening up a new market for your company
- checking whether your company has the time and staff resources to prepare and write the proposal.

After you have considered these points you (or your company management) should then be able to decide

(a)   whether or not to submit a proposal
(b)   which project staff to use from your company

(c)   which partner companies to work with
(d)   which company is to take the lead in preparing the proposal.

Summary: the preliminary review

- Don't decide to write a proposal simply because you've been invited to: it's not always worthwhile — think about it first.
- Write to the client confirming that you will (or maybe, will not after all) send him a proposal by the stated submission date.
- Read the TOR: understand clearly what the client is looking for, and what his evaluation system is.
- Define the tasks which you will have to carry out during the project: start a task list.
- Collect background information; make a site visit. You need local knowledge.
- Identify what the client's priorities will be in selecting the successful consultant.
- Note what key staff the project tasks call for.
- Decide whether you want to work with other companies in carrying out the new project — unusual partner companies can give your proposal a political or regional balance.
- If your company is submitting a joint proposal, decide which company will take the lead in preparing the proposals document.
- Identify the proposals leader.

Start-up

This involves

- proposals team
- proposals programme
- proposals office
- proposals budget.

This is the stage where you get organised. Do not make the mistake of jumping straight from the preliminary review to writing text. Few successful consultants would take this approach to a project bringing US$300 000 of fees, and that is about the equivalent of a typical international proposal (proposals costs compared with project fees). Your company should set up an organisation to work on the proposal, set limits on the costs the organisation may incur, agree a programme to complete the proposal, and provide the facilities which the organisation will need to do so. The reasons for these four steps are

- *Proposals team.* Very few people can prepare a proposal by themselves: some may be able to describe the engineering services but cannot type or use graphics software; others might be able to describe the country-specific problems but not the technical ones. Even if someone actually could do all the work themselves, they probably couldn't do it alone in the time available.
- *Proposals budget.* Companies will have agreed to spend money on the proposal, simply by deciding to submit one; but they will probably decide not to spend more money than they are likely to make from the project. Companies need to specify a figure within this range so that the proposals team can develop its work programme (for example, how long should the site visit be and who should make it). The decision on the proposals budget should relate to the company's risk investment programme, which in turn should be part of its marketing strategy. Few engineering consultants organise themselves as well as this, and there are even some who do not monitor proposal costs at all.
- *Proposals programme.* It is possible to break down any task into a series of steps, which have to proceed in a sensible order and to an overall time plan — this is a basic part of good project management. You need to do the same when setting out to write a proposal.
- *Proposals office.* This item covers the facilities you will need to prepare the proposal, such as a room to work in, computers, colour printing facilities, E-mail links, and refreshments (most proposals eventually involve people working long hours).

The following notes discuss these steps in more detail.

Proposals team

Writing technical and financial proposals usually demands a range of skills rarely found in one person. Proposals for international projects need the support of even more experts than those for large, home-country projects. For example, the team for an international proposal will need a country expert; if your own company's base is a non-English speaking country then your team will need translators and multilingual technical staff (the language of most international proposals is English); and if the TOR asks for the proposals to be submitted in more than one language you will probably need several translators.

The various people who can help write the proposal fall into one of four groups: the core team, specialists, short-term support, and company links. Some of the key members will sooner or later will be working on it almost full-time. These people include the team leader and the support staff, and form the *core team*. The core team will need the help of other *specialists* from time-to-time during their work — experts in secondary areas of the work (for example, environmental experts for a rural road design project), and someone representing the company management (who can guarantee them extra resources when there is a competing demand for them). The third group includes *short-term support* staff such as translators, legal advisors and quality assurance readers. If your firm has decided to associate with others for this project, then these companies will provide some of the technical specialists, and perhaps the country expert (otherwise, there would be no need to associate with other companies). Partner firms have to nominate people to act as the *links* between themselves and the proposals team — to guarantee the prompt supply of details for the financial proposal, for example.

Selecting the key members of the proposal team If your company is to lead the work on the proposal then it should provide the proposals team leader — not least because the lead company usually has to carry most of the expense. Your company will also have to supply most of the support staff. Deciding which company provides the other team members will depend on what their particular strengths are, and on how you decide to split the work (and the costs). The composition of the proposals team also depends on the size and type of the project and on the size of the proposals budget.

There is one other basic selection process which you must consider. If you want to produce a very good proposal you will need *new* team members, people who are prepared to carry out a range of tasks without complaining, who will work overtime when it is necessary, and who do not insist on sticking to traditional, out-of-date roles. The following notes in Table 21 describe the new team members (see also checklist 12). Table 22 describes the old, out-of-date type of team member.

Table 21. Members of the new proposals team

Team member	Description
Core team	
Team leader	The team leader is responsible for seeing that the technical and financial proposals are ready on time and within the budget, and that they agree with each other. He should have worked overseas, be an expert in at least one of the areas which the project involves, and have the authority to take decisions on his own. The team leader should be computer-literate, capable of typing his own text, and aware of at least the basics of computer graphics and project-management software. In addition he should have good person-management skills and • involve the other team members in the project • ask his colleagues to work over-time only when it's necessary • share any credit and accepts any blame.
Technical writer	Documents need one author. The technical writer has to make sure that the documents are clearly presented, easy to read, have a consistent style, and actually answer the questions which the TOR set out. He also should have worked overseas, and be an expert in at least one of the areas which the project involves. Where possible the technical writer and the team leader should be the same person. The writer must • be able to type his own text • be familiar with computer graphics and project-management software . . .
General support	This person should be able to carry out research, arrange meetings, help organise other staff, look after computer files, and use word-processing, spreadsheet and a variety of other software (not — *use* means more than just typing). He should also be able to • think for himself • stay calm during a crisis • use E-mail • speak English (and ideally at least one other language).
Graphics support	Good presentation may win only 2% of the points in the formal evaluation system (Table 19) but it will earn a lot more in goodwill from the people who have to read the documents. This will show through in the final results. Good presentation itself depends on clearly-presented tables, charts and other graphics. The person who prepares the graphics should • have a good sense of combining colour, layout and text • be able to use a range of graphics programs.
Country expert	The country expert should have a good feel for the country and its people; he should know something about the country's history, society and politics; and ideally his local contacts should include people in the client's organisation. This person might be your company's

Table 21.   continued

Team member	Description
	regional or country representative, or someone from your local partner company (if you have one). He should also • be able to use E-mail and a word-processor • have a technical/engineering background.
Specialists Technical experts	These people provide the high-value technical input to the proposal. They should be aware of the latest international techniques in their area of expertise (which, for international proposals, means more than familiar with modern techniques in their *own* country). They should know what techniques are commonly used in the target country, and what special requirements other interested parties may have (for example, some banks have published their own guidelines on environmental impact studies). Technical experts should also • preferably have worked overseas • be able to type and prepare their own reports.
Businessman	Someone has to decide which potential partner companies to team up with, which people to select for the project team, how much to charge the client for profit and fees (and how to distribute costs among the company's accounts), what special offers might be included in the proposal for no extra charge, and so on. The businessman should be familiar with your firm's international marketing strategy and with its overall business development strategy. He should also ideally • have a technical background • have worked overseas • have some experience in marketing.
Management support	Every proposal brings the occasional, unexpected crisis — a partner company decides to team up with the opposition, a team member falls sick, or you suddenly need two extra computers. As team leader you need some management support. The person nominated should be a member of middle management of the company, versed in the team-work approach to management ('those who can do, those who manage, help them do it') and in the cooperation theory of problem solving ('you've got a crisis — let's work out how can we solve it'). The person involved should • be available as required, particularly during the core stage (at which time he is needed to support the principle that work on the proposal takes priority over everything else) • be responsible for the success of the company's international activities.
Project management expert	This person is able to provide the analytical links between project activities, resources, resource consumption, costs, and time planning. He does not need to have worked overseas or be a technical expert — but it would help. He should certainly be able to use standard project management software.
Accountant	Someone very familiar with your company's bookkeeping and accounts, he should be able to provide the detailed information

Table 21. continued

Team member	Description
	and technical support which you will need during preparation of the financial proposal document (e.g. details of insurance cover, social costs and overhead charges).

Short-term support

The legal advisor	The legal advisor should check the details of association arrangements (whether with potential joint venture partners, sub-consultants or freelance staff), bearing in mind the need to define responsibilities and the allocation of risk and liability; he should review any contracts prepared by the client, advise on arrangements for arbitration and mediation both between the members of the joint venture, and between the joint venture and the client.
Translator	Someone who translates the written word: necessary when the proposal documents have to be submitted in more than one language; or when some of the background documents are only available in the language of the target country (the TOR for international projects are usually issued in English). A translator may also be needed where the proposal team's technical experts cannot write in English.
Interpreter	Someone who translates the spoken word: necessary during business meetings and presentations where the client's representatives cannot speak good English. In these cases he should be familiar with the main selling points of the proposal.
VIP	A member of the company's upper or middle management, he prepares his client (or country) visits in discussion with the country representative/expert and with the proposals team leader. Further, <ul><li>in meetings with local contacts attended by his representative, he allows the representative to take the lead role</li><li>he allows himself to be used as a problem solver: gives advice on strategic decisions; and, acting on the advice of the representative, visits a client either to soothe ruffled feathers or to impress him with his (the clients') importance.</li></ul>
Technical QA	Someone has to read the final drafts of the technical and financial proposals to check that they are understandable, consistent and make (technical) sense. Whoever does it should have a technical background and some experience in either writing or evaluating proposals. He should not be a member of the core proposals team — no-one can properly check their own work.
Style QA	This person has to check that the style of the proposal documents are consistent, he should make edit checks such as correct page numbering, consistent table layout, heading styles, text layout and font type and size etc. This person should also preferably not be a member of the core team.
Company links	People nominated by your partner companies to act aslinks between themselves and you as team leader for the proposal.

Table 21. continued

Team member	Description
	These people should have some interest in the proposal, seniority in their company, and preferably both overseas and technical experience.
General	Desirably all team members should have worked together before, and • be flexible: prepared to do menial tasks such as photocopying and tea-making, as well as providing their own, more technical input . . . • speak English, and preferably one other language.

Proposals programme

Engineering construction projects always involve a number of different but related tasks; these tasks have to be completed in order and the whole project has to be completed on time. To ensure this you as project engineer would prepare a work programme for it. Preparing a proposal is exactly the same. It too, involves a number of related tasks which have to be completed in order, and the project has to be completed on time.

Setting out a proposals programme will help you and the rest of the proposals team understand the tasks involved and successfully carry them out — which in turn means that the proposal has a good chance of becoming a successful new project.

Proposals quality and programme time Books on project management often discuss the *quality — cost — time* triangle. They explain that increasing the emphasis on one side of the triangle will have a negative effect on the other sides. For example, demanding an increase in quality will probably mean that the project will need more staff (costs) and take longer to complete (time). Proposals are a little different, in that the time available for preparing them is always fixed and inflexible, and it usually makes business sense to put an upper limit on costs. Quality takes a reluctant third place.

You will have to rely on indirect sources of quality assurance for the work on the proposal. For example, a small team of people with experience of working together on proposals is usually better than a large team of individual experts who have never worked on them.

There are a number of causes for the fixed time factor. The TOR specify the date the documents have to be submitted by — perhaps two months after the date the client issued the LOI. Of course, you will never have the two months to prepare the documents. You will lose a week or two at the beginning of this period while someone

Table 22. Brief characteristics of members of the old out-of-date proposals team

Team member	Description
Core team	
Team leader	Someone more prepared to allocate work to the team members, less prepared to do any real work himself; a person with limited overseas experience, and less experience of working with computers.
Technical writer	The average British engineer: often unable to type or use a word-processor, and incapable of writing clear, concise, readable text.
General support	Secretary — typist, capable of taking dictation, typing with word-processing software, and answering telephone calls. Usually only available to the team leader; someone who prefers to wait for instructions.
Graphics support	Technical draughtsman, able to use a drawing board and colour pencils.
Country expert	Someone who is too busy travelling as a regional salesman to provide any useful input to the proposals team.
Specialists	
Technical experts	Generally unaware of any techniques in their area of expertise besides those they learnt at university, and not particularly interested in finding out.
Businessman	An exponent of one style of butterfly management, flying from country to country without (a) finding out what information the proposals team needs before departing and (b) without telling them anything useful on his return.
Management support	Member of middle management of the company, versed in the top – down approach to management and in the delegation theory of crisis-solving.
Project management expert	Not usually included in the old team; other members would prepare details of manning schedules, work programmes and cost, in the hope that the reviewer would find them plausible. The proposals team would leave the project staff to solve any problems of implementing the project on the basis of these schedules. Of course, if things did not actually work out on-site then that would be due to the incompetence of the project staff.
Short-term support	
Legal advisor	Not usually included in the old team; the other team members assumed, for example, that 'joint and several liability' meant that each member of the joint venture could be held responsible only for his share of the work involved.
Translator, interpreter	Not usually included in the old team.
VIP	A member of the company's upper or middle management, he makes his own high-level contacts with the client or in the country of interest; he does not bother to check either before or after with the company's representative for that client (or country).

Table 22. continued

Team member	Description
QA checks	Both formerly left to the technical writer.
Company links	People nominated by other companies to provide support for the proposals team; chosen because they have nothing else to do at the time, and so often with even less interest in the proposal.

decides whether your company should submit a proposal at all; and you will lose a week or more at the end of the period in the time it will take to deliver the documents. It is worthwhile setting out the key programme dates before doing anything else

- date TOR issued
- date TOR received
- *date decision made to submit a proposal*
- *date documents have to be posted*

$\left. \begin{array}{l} \\ \\ \end{array} \right\} = actual\ time\ available$

- date documents have to be submitted by.

The most important of these is the submission date. The dominating rule is that the documents *must* be submitted on time — it is better to submit imperfect documents by the submission date than perfect documents two days later.

Pressures, efficiency and availability A second triangle, less often discussed in project management textbooks, is the *pressure — efficiency — work load* triangle. Pressure is a measure of the stress someone is working under. Usually people in a consultancy are involved in a number of different projects at the same time, and so a more useful measure is relevant pressure. This is an indication of the stress someone is working under and which is due to their involvement in your proposal. When people are under no pressure for your project they do no work for it; when pushed beyond their maximum pressure they break down and again do not work efficiently. Some people will remember this from their experience of studying for school examinations: first of all they didn't study because there was so much time left; then they panicked (and didn't study) because there was so little time left.

Efficiency is an indication of the quality of the work people are producing. Both efficiency and pressure are related to availability. If someone is only working part-time for your project then he will be under less stress to produce any results. You will also be competing for his interest and (by definition) cannot hope to have it all: he will certainly not be working efficiently, at least so far as your proposal is concerned. When the same person is available to work on your proposal full-time but you don't have much for him to do — then again, he will be under less stress and will work less efficiently.

As team leader for the proposal your task will be to produce a balance between the pressure, efficiency and availability curves (Fig. 7). This is quite easy.

- The pressure increases substantially during the last three or four weeks of the proposal programme, simply because there is little time left to do the work and solve any problems which arise (and even if the supervising agency allowed an extra month for the programme, most consultants would not make any use of the extra time).
- People can usually work at maximum efficiency for a couple of weeks, which is about the period of maximum pressure for a proposal. You should not try to put them under artificial pressure at the start of the programme, since this will only lead to early burn out.
- You need to plan full-time availability of the core team for times when you have a crisis, crises are problems which occur when there is no time left to solve them, and that happens (by definition) at the end of the programme period.
- Your team can only work full-time after completing the background research. This phase will take the first two to four weeks of the programme itself.

Programmes — the human factor   These days people use computers to help them with all sorts of activities. In proposals, engineers use them for word-processing, estimating costs, preparing charts and graphics, and so on. The engineers ask special advisors to make sure that the various programs, the computers, printers and other hardware, are compatible with each other. If they are not compatible then the system breaks down and the proposal will be in trouble. As the proposals team leader you will have the same problems with the individuals who make up the proposals team. Here also, if they are not compatible, the system breaks down and the proposal will be in trouble. Your company is unlikely to have special advisors to help you sort out this type of problem however, even though interpersonal relationships — the human factor — probably account for more than 50% of the element of success or failure in a project. As one book on project management notes

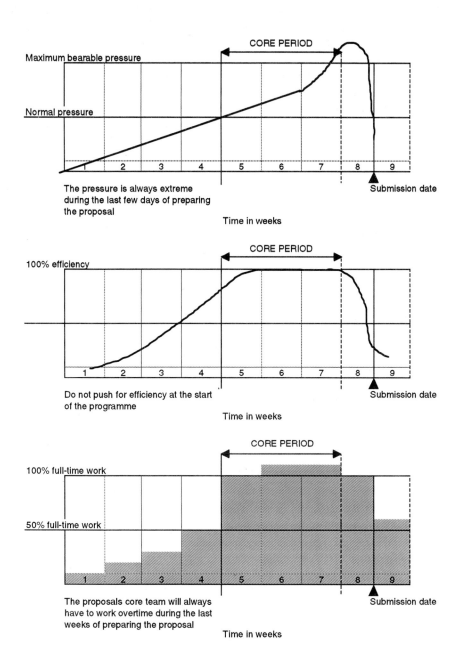

Fig. 7. Pressure and efficiency in preparing proposals

> Seldom is a lack of planning or control the main cause for a badly-running project; its failure is much more often caused by an unsuitable project organisation and by *difficulties in the relations between the people involved* (and other human problems) . . .[34]

and

> Such problems can have a number of different causes (for example uninterested managers who bother themselves too little with the problems of the project, weak team leaders or demotivated team members, etc.)[35]

You will probably not have much say in the selection of the members for the proposals team, but you *will* be responsible for whatever they eventually produce. Here are a some points on how to deal with the human side of your project (gathered from experience gained on both sides of the fence).

- Treat even the most unimportant member of the team with some respect, if for no other reason than that even the most unimportant member can help screw up the proposal.
- Try and develop a proposals team made up of people who are used to working together under stress. It is better to have a team with perhaps average skills, but common understanding, than a team of highly-specialised individuals.
- When you want to shout at someone on your team for his incompetence, go out for a walk and a cup of coffee. It takes seconds to destroy a working relationship, but months to build it up again. In proposals, you just don't have months available.
- Listen to even the silliest suggestions which people in your team make — sooner or later they will come up with a good idea.
- Don't shift the deadlines — people psychologically prepare themselves for the maximum pressure as a target date approaches. Moving the deadline has the same effect as completing the work, in that the release of pressure leads to a catastrophic (for you) fall in efficiency (Fig. 7).

---

34 *Projektmanagement — Methoden, Techniken, Verhaltensweisen*, by Hans-D. Litke, published by Carl Hanser Verlag, Munich 1991, page 13 (own translation and emphasis).

35 *Projektmanagement — Methoden, Techniken, Verhaltensweisen*, by Hans-D. Litke, published by Carl Hanser Verlag, Munich 1991, page 40 (own translation).

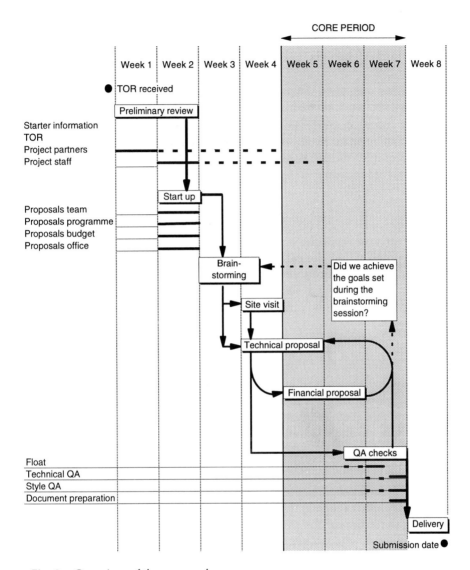

Fig. 8. Overview of the proposals programme

- Keep a sense of proportion.
- Try and make your colleagues feel like a team — give them specific responsibilities, have them meet regularly (even for just five minutes).
- If the team members work for different companies and are based in different cities, bring them together for a joint meeting at the start of the work. The official reason may be to brainstorm, the real reason is that they should get to know each other as valuable individuals.

- In the last days of a proposal pressure can be quite severe, and people can become short-tempered — you should allow for it.

Programme overview Every project and every proposal has its own peculiarities, and so you should prepare your own detailed programme for each proposal. Having said that, it is still possible to provide an outline programme which will apply to every proposal you will come across, however large or small. Fig. 8 assumes that there are two months to prepare the proposal.

Proposals office

Once you have volunteered to be the team leader for the proposal and have identified the other members of the team, you will be able to decide which room in which building should be the project headquarters — the 'project office'. The advantages of such a room are that you have

(a) somewhere to keep project-related material such as document drafts and plans
(b) somewhere for informal team meetings
(c) somewhere where you and the other members of the core team can work undisturbed
(d) and not least, somewhere which gives the proposals project a sense of physical identity.

A special office is not necessary if the proposal is very simple. Otherwise you should try to obtain the use of a room at least for the core period of preparing the proposal. It should be in the building where you normally work, since as team leader you at least, should have an overview of the proposals. It could be your usual office, but if you share it with someone else your colleague may want to move out during the core period. The disturbance and noise which you and the other team members make then will probably be too much for him to bear.

Proposals office facilities You and the other team members will also need some special facilities and equipment to help you work efficiently. The proposals office will be the best place to keep much of it. The facilities include

- *Standard computer hardware and software.* Everyone uses computer facilities these days; your problem is to make sure that you and the other members of the proposals team use the same facilities. For example, you will face problems if one partner company uses Macintoshes, another uses PC's with MS-Word, and a third uses PC's with WordPerfect.

- *A proposals library.* You should begin the background research by collecting material such as

   ○ copies of previous proposals which your company prepared for projects in the target country
   ○ copies of previous proposals which your company prepared for the financing institution
   ○ project-related reports such as feasibility studies, local design manuals
   ○ correspondence files and other proposals documentation
   ○ tourist guides to the target country (for team members who have never been there)
   ○ company brochures from your partner firms.

- *Spare desk and computer.* For visiting team members.
- *Wall maps.* Showing the location and physical background to the project.
- *Laying-out tables.* Somewhere to keep the working drafts of the proposal documents, for sorting copied pages, and for use as informal conference tables.
- *Tea and coffee-making facilities.* When you have to work twelve hours a day the extra caffeine will help keep you going. Tea or coffee can also be an excuse to sit down with other team members and review progress, and can help calm people down after an argument. For a proposals office these could be classed as medically-recommended facilities.

Proposals budget

Submitting a proposal is like betting on a horse race: the odds are against you. Your proposal has a theoretical 1 in 6 chance of winning, although you can increase your chances by studying the form (background knowledge) — and sooner or later you have to decide how much money to wager. You can risk a little or a lot. In proposal's for example, your company may decide not to bother with a site visit, or to send a high-level team including the company chairman. The decision on a budget limit for the proposal has to be made by your company management. They should refer to their marketing strategy, and ask the opinion of their regional representative and the proposals team leader (the proposals team leader is unlikely to be the budget holder). There is no point in someone complaining afterwards about the cost of a proposal if they did not set a limit for it beforehand.

Very often a consultant will team up with partner companies for a particular proposal. Each partner will have an idea of the fees it is likely to make from the desired project, and should be prepared to pay its share of the costs of bidding for it. The careful partner should ask for an estimate of the costs of the proposal before work starts on it, and a statement of expense incurred after the documents have been submitted. As team leader you may not have an estimate of the likely costs of a proposal, or keep a record of the costs actually incurred. In this case there can be no suggestion of charging partner

Table 23. Costs of preparing a proposal

Task/activity	Detail note	Income US$	Outlay US$
Marketing (1)	Marketing — covered in company overheads	–	–
Invitation	Marketing — covered in company overheads[*]	–	–
Background research			
Staff costs	Professional (average 1 person–month)[†]		10 000
	Support (average 1 person–month)[‡]		4000
Other costs	Brainstorming (travel and accommodation)	–	1000
	Site visit (travel and accommodation)[§]	–	2000
Administration	Telephone, fax, E-mail, paper etc.	–	500
Core period			
Staff costs	Professional (average 1 person–month)[†]		10 000
	Support (average 1 person–month)[‡]		4000
Other costs	Submission (colour printing, courier etc.)		1000
Administration	Telephone, fax, E-mail, paper etc.	–	500
Follow-up	Marketing–covered in company overheads	–	–
Marketing (2)	Marketing–covered in company overheads	–	–
		none	$33 000

Assumptions.
[*] Invitation costs (EOI, PQ etc.) included in company overheads.
[†] Professional staff salary = US$4000 per month (+ social charges at 30%, overheads at 120%).
[‡] Support staff salary = US$1600 per month + social charges at 30%, overheads at 120%).
[§] Site visit takes ten days, one person makes the site visit.

Notes.
- Assuming a profit rate of 15% on remuneration, then the costs of a typical proposal (from the above table) represent the income from a successful project worth $220 000.
- The table does not include for costs of any local incentives.
- The table is meant to indicate of the scale of potential costs; you should prepare your own table for your proposal/project.

Table 24. Income from a successful project

Task/activity	Detail note	Income US$	Outlay US$
Total income		1 200 000	
of which costs			
Out-of-pocket	Out-of-pocket expenses		200 000
Remuneration	Salary costs		353 000
	Overheads at 120% of salary costs		424 000
	Social charges at 30% of salary costs		106 000
	Backstopping (covered in overheads)	–	–
Fee/profit	Fees (15% of salary costs and overheads)		117 000
		1 200 000	1 200 000

Notes.
The table is meant to indicate the scale of costs and fees/profits; you should prepare your own table for your proposal/project.

companies for their share of the costs, and no complaints about overstepping a budget — but it certainly doesn't make business sense.

Proposals budgets should have two parts: forecast costs and (later) the incurred costs. The most sensible way to estimate both is to record the same sort of information that you will include in the financial proposal (Tables 23 and 24). Your company management may decide to discount such items as the costs of secretaries' time, courier shipments and colour printing — but that should be an informed decision, and not one made in blind ignorance.

In summary, the reasons for preparing a proposals budget are

- in advance of the proposal, to give an idea of the financial resources available for the work
- post-proposal, to help your company control the costs of their international marketing strategy
- to identify areas for potential cost savings
- to allow proposal costs to be shared between partner companies.

Brainstorming meeting

Brainstorming is a practical example of the advice to 'think before you act'. People involved directly or just on the fringes of the proposal meet to discuss ideas ranging from *how to prepare the proposal documents* to *how to carry out the actual project*. The results will allow you and the proposals team to learn from the past mistakes, and produce a convincing technical approach to the work involved in the project. The brainstorming meeting also has an important, if indirect, benefit: it gives the proposals team members an opportunity to get to know each other, and to do so before the pressure builds up.

You can't brainstorm alone — you need other people. The meeting should include at least three people (the team leader, the businessman and the engineer), preferably all the members of the core proposals team, and (ideally) the technical specialists and people from the partner companies as well as the company links. Inviting a secretary to such a discussion may seem strange, but she will probably know more than anyone else about problems of document production and delivery. Their inclusion will also help the team-building process.

The best time to hold the brainstorming meeting is

- *after* reviewing the TOR, preparing a task list, and outlining the proposals programme (so that you have something to talk about)
- *after* deciding on project partners and the proposals team (so that you have someone to talk with)
- *before* the site visit (so that the site visit isn't a complete waste of time).

Brainstorming agenda A meeting without an agenda is a failure from the start. An agenda for this particular type of brainstorming meeting should cover the following points

- *Background research*

  ○ pool background knowledge of the country
  ○ pool background knowledge of the client
  ○ pool background knowledge of the funding agency
  ○ identify gaps in background knowledge

- *The proposal*

  ○ review the proposals programme
  ○ agree on the proposals team
  ○ agree on cost-sharing
  ○ agree on task allocation
  ○ agree on basics (e.g. computer software, document text styles, contact numbers and names)

- *The project*
  - ○ review the draft project task list
  - ○ discuss the technical approach and methodology
  - ○ look for new ideas on how to carry out the project.

Outputs from the brainstorming meeting The main results from the brainstorming meeting should include a detailed list of questions for the site visit, and agreement on the proposals programme. Important outputs relating more directly to the project include a revised task list, revised key staff list, and some agreement on the approach and methodology to be used. Perhaps, most importantly, the brainstorming meeting should come up with ideas which will make your team win the project.

Site visit

However well equipped your proposals library may be, and however experienced your proposals team, you are unlikely to collect all the background information you need about the new project from sitting in your home office. If your company is really interested in the work, sooner or later someone will have to make a site visit. This will probably be the first time that you or another member of the proposals team actually set foot on the physical location of the new work. Visiting the client's office and having a relaxed conversation with him is no substitute (for example) for a drive along the route of a proposed rural road improvement scheme. The main purpose of the exercise is to bring the added value of local knowledge. This will allow you to describe the way in which your company would carry out the proposed services in terms of the client's particular problems, background and society. Without it, the technical proposal notes will read like abstract textbook theory. More pragmatic reasons for the site visit are to collect further details on local costs, the client's evaluation priorities, and so on.

Who should make the site visit? The person who makes the site visit should be a member of the proposals team. In order of preference he should be

- someone with regional and project-related technical experience
- the proposals team leader
- a lead technical expert from the proposals team
- the area representative
- the local partner.

The local partner will already have background local knowledge (of course); but he probably will not be able to see the project from the viewpoint of a technical expert.

Purposes of the site visit The main purpose for the site visit is to help fill in the gaps in the proposals team's background knowledge. It should therefore take place after the brainstorming meeting, which is supposed to identify these gaps. There are two other purposes to bear in mind. The first is getting to know the staff of the local partner company. Assuming this isn't a one-proposal relationship (which it shouldn't be if you have developed a sensible marketing strategy) then these personal contacts should lead to increased efficiency on all other future joint studies. The second is to show the client that you are seriously interested in his project. It is the only reason where a visit by someone from your company management could make sense.

Check list 10 suggests some questions for the site visit.

Reducing the costs of proposals

Table 23 suggests that proposals can cost the consultant over $30 000. This is roughly $30 000 more than most companies would like to pay. You will win friends if you can suggest ways which will reduce costs — and preferably without affecting the quality. Here are some possibilities.

Proposals team

Smaller teams Smaller, simpler proposals will need fewer resources, but this doesn't necessarily reduce the size of the proposals team. The only way to achieve this without a significant loss of quality is by combining different skills in fewer people. As one example, the team leader should also be a technical expert, and preferably the technical writer. It would also help if all the technical staff were able to type and proofread their own text. Unfortunately many engineers consider using a word-processor to be a skill fit only for subordinate staff.

The smallest team has two members, both engineers or experts. One person alone cannot prepare a good proposal: he will always need an informed listener to discuss his ideas with, and he will rarely be able to cope with the pressures of the core period by himself.

Standard core team In every field of human activity, people get better with practice. Wherever possible you should use the same people in the core team. They will learn from their own mistakes, and increase their productivity with every proposal they work on. This does not mean that they should work together even when they haven't a proposal to work on, however. . . .

Permanent core team One way of overcoming the problems of the human factor is for people to work successfully together under stress — which is the case with most proposals. It would be a pity not to use this side-benefit by employing the team on other projects. They could for example, work on the preparation of standard material such as project references and staff CVs.

Standard Partner Companies Teamwork between companies improves with practice (which is not surprising, since companies are simply groups of people). For this reason you should select partner companies with a long-term view in mind.

Proposals programme

Start early A sensible idea but one which for some reason never works; but it's one way of avoiding the crisis of running out of time — and the expense of throwing staff into the work to overcome it.

Finish early — by creating an artificial deadline: this is another sensible idea for avoiding a crisis, but also one which doesn't seem to work in practice.

Make decisions more quickly The longer it takes someone to decide to go ahead with the proposal, the less time is available to prepare it calmly and efficiently.

Proposals Budget

Smaller Teams Using smaller teams, the idea of a permanent core team etc. will help reduce costs as well as time.

Less-qualified staff You will need at least two key technical staff on the proposal, but much of the work can be done by less-qualified (and less expensive) support staff. Your company should establish a basic supply of standard material such as company project references, key staff CVs etc. This could be reworked for each proposal by the general support staff member(s) of the proposal team.

Proposals Office

E-Mail Use of E-mail and the Internet seems like an ideal way to exchange draft text and graphics between the different offices and companies which may be involved in the proposal. Unfortunately there is still a large gap between theory and practice. Few people can use E-mail, and they are usually on holiday when you need them; and the different companies probably use incompatible software. Don't rely on E-mail; but if you do decide to exchange data electronically, mark in colour the paragraphs containing text corrections or new text, otherwise the document author cannot see what you have changed. (He can see the colour on the screen but it doesn't mean he has to print a colour version of the text).

Pre-prepared material Some material is common to all proposals: examples are the general description of the company, and project references. The more you can employ these sort of notes, then the less time you need to spend writing from scratch.

Standard styles Two people usually have two opinions about text and graphic style (style covers questions such as: should the page numbers be on the bottom left or the bottom right of the page; should text be in Arial or Helvetica font). The value of pre-prepared material is also reduced if the new team leader decides to use a different font style or size. Your company should have its own style guide, which it should require all its employees to use. Owning (and actually using) a good style manual can also impress your partner firms.

Move to a new room People who work on a proposal from their normal office will be constantly disrupted by their regular colleagues, their boss, and by telephone calls unrelated to the proposal. Disruption leads to delay. It can take 30-minutes to recover from even a five-minute conversation about other work. Particularly during the core period, they should be offered a desk in another room some distance removed from their usual one.

Work from home — still too new for some consultants (who trust staff to work unobserved from the office, but do not trust them to work unobserved from home) the idea is particularly useful for the technical writer.

Brainstorming meeting

Telephone-based meetings If you are working with people you already know (from your own and from any partner companies) you may be able to replace a physical meeting with a telephone-based meeting or teleconference. This is particularly valid for smaller proposals, or where time is short.

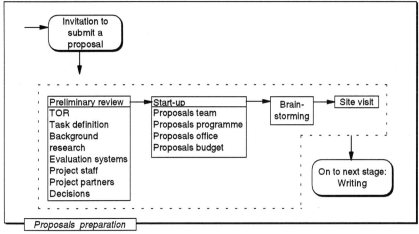

TASK INPUT

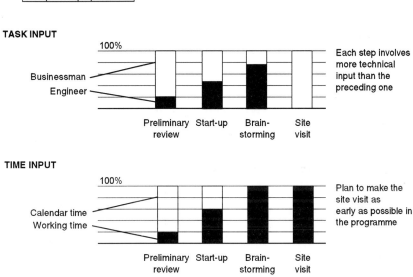

TIME INPUT

Fig. 9.   Proposals preparation

Site visit

Cancel the site visit — or have the local partner make it: a possibility where members of the proposals team have considerable regional experience, but one which is always likely to reduce the quality of the proposal, and is **not** a good idea.

Summary

Preparing to write a proposal is probably the most important link in the whole chain of events leading up to submitting the completed documents, and probably also the one treated most carelessly. It marks the boundary between the activities where the businessman dominates and those where the engineer dominates. Successful cooperation here will provide a rock-solid basis for the written proposal. In the less successful consultants the business/engineering split is so strong that neither side bothers to look after the other's interests. The proposal preparation will be weak, and the written proposal will quickly sink out of sight. For further notes see below and Fig. 9.

- Read the TOR (and then read them again).
- Before deciding to proceed with the proposal, compare time and costs of preparing proposal with the likely profits to be made.
- Check the time needed for document preparation and delivery, and treat it as fixed.
- Don't aim for perfection — a good proposal delivered on time is better than a perfect proposal delivered two days too late.
- Try to aim for a completion date at least three days before the absolute last possible completion date.
- Plan the CV activity from day 1 of the programme (see later chapters).
- Keep a draft copy of the proposal documents from the first day of the programme.
- Remember that some partner companies are seemingly less reliable than your own (they have less to lose).
- Brainstorming — think first.
- Get organised — set up a proposals team/budget/programmes and office.
- If you make a site visit, try and bring back something useful.
- Always allow 1–2 days to review and correct text (QA work). This is not a float and you should not treat it as such.
- Keep track of proposals costs (e.g. using an accounts system/time sheets).
- Note that it can take from one to two hours to translate one A4 page of technical text.
- Start with a brainstorming session.
- Visit the client.
- Submit the proposal on time.
- Start the proposal on time.
- Allow time for errors.

6

Writing technical proposals

Introduction

After all the work of marketing and acquisition, you and your proposals team can now get down to the task of actually writing the proposal documents. The Terms of Reference normally ask consultants to submit two documents

(a)   a technical proposal and
(b)   a financial proposal.

The evaluation process may then cover just the technical proposal (leaving the financial part to form the basis of negotiations between the client and the consultant). Alternatively, it might be a two-stage process involving weighted assessment of the technical — perhaps 85% — *plus* the financial — 15% — proposals. In both cases, the consultants post off the two parts in separate, sealed envelopes.[36] It makes sense to start with the technical proposal, since without it you have nothing to base the cost estimates on.

Before pen meets paper, you should consider some basic details of working on the proposal documents: **techniques, methodology administration** and **style**.

Techniques

There are various ways of developing a written proposal. You can concentrate on describing the novel technical applications that you

---

36 FIDIC *Guidelines on quality-based selection of consulting engineers*, page 7, 1991. EU Phare standard tender documents, para. B.3; etc.

would introduce to the project, or you might want to approach the work from the point-of-view of a project manager. Some techniques are more popular among engineers than others — but then, popularity never won any medals.

Copying text Most companies have some experience of writing international proposals, and will have a store of old proposal documents. These usually cover either the same subject area or the same region, as the proposal you are involved in now. Since writing completely original text can seem like one of the more difficult labours of Hercules, you may want to copy some of the material from the previous documents. The danger is that the original proposal failed because it was poorly written; or perhaps the text refers to local circumstances which no longer apply. In copying old text, you risk using material which was defective, or past its sell-by date. Careless copying and editing can also lead to geographic blunders such as referring to 'the Ganges, one of Vietnam's largest rivers', making it obvious to the reader what you have been up to.

Other original material, such as textbooks and technical journals, can provide useful supporting text. Quoting from a manual on pavement management can support the management approach you propose to use provided you acknowledge the source. Never underestimate the client by quoting from published sources and pretending the work is your own; he will probably be more familiar with the original than you are.

Use of modules Most proposals cover the same main points: company descriptions for example, or notes on technology transfer, backstopping, environmental protection, and so on. Once you have written (or have found from earlier documents) a *genuinely useful* piece of text in any of these areas, you should put a copy away for future use. These stored modules can be used either as part of the main text or as special side notes to it.

Methodology

Technology-based There is a tendency for engineers to be interested in engineering. You will probably be in a rush to use the technical proposal to demonstrate your engineering experience to the client. You will also be eager to explain the new ideas which you would be pleased to apply, should he be sensible enough to award the project to your company. This technology-based way of developing the technical proposal may deeply satisfy you but it will not necessarily satisfy the client. Formal evaluation systems score only 3% for innovation, for example (see chapter 5). This method may be more suited to private sector clients.

Task-based This technique treats the proposal as if it were a project-management guide for the new scheme. It identifies

- the tasks to be carried out, as requested in the TOR
- the resources needed for each task (time, key personnel, support staff, local facilities)
- the sequence which the tasks need to be carried out in (the work programme)
- the outputs from each task (completed reports, field surveys, traffic counts etc).

This seems to be the way things are going (recent TOR from one IFI has even asked for critical path charts) but it can present the proposals team with a number of disadvantages. First, it makes it much more clear to the client what he will be getting for his money. Second, more parts of the technical proposal are interdependent: changes in one part will force you to make changes in several others. Third, it makes it more difficult for the proposals team to bluff, for example by producing a work-programme chart which looks very impressive but whose details in fact imply that the project manager has to spend most of his time working 30 hours a day, and in two different places at the same time.

The technique also has several advantages: it makes it clear to the specialists on the proposals team what they have to describe and cost for, and it will produce more dependable project cost estimates and work programmes.

Failure-based approach The do-minimum technique is to identify the main tasks from the TOR and then quote (again from the TOR) to describe what these main tasks will involve. Lack of originality, boredom and sheer cheek are likely to earn your proposal minimum points. If the client wanted a proposal like this, he would have written it himself.

Suggested approach The task-based approach should be the preferred basic technique for most proposals, with modules and a limited amount of free text providing the supporting material. The tasks, plus the structure of the technical proposal (see below) will form the framework or skeleton of the proposal. Modules and freetext put the flesh on the bones. One idea of the relative proportions of these approaches is shown in Table 25.

From it you can see that use of modules may save you 40% of your time, which you can use either to improve the work programme and cost estimates, or to save on proposals costs.

Administration

Administration is an activity which has earned itself a bad name in recent years. It has become synonymous with such negative charac- teristics as delay, obstruction and mindless paper-shuffling. Perhaps we should use an alternative name, such as housekeeping. The word suggests the ideas of good order, tidiness and efficiency, and that is what the *administration* of the technical proposal is all about. It covers a number of the following activities.

Master copy You should keep a master copy of the technical pro- posal as soon as you begin to work on it. At first it will be nothing more than a hardback folder with a few divider sheets in it. Later on it will contain the latest drafts of text, as well as colour drafts of graphics and charts (black-and-white drafts of any colour pages do not really show how understandable they are, nor do they help give the right impression of the overall document). The advantages of keeping an up-to-date master copy are that

- everyone involved can follow progress on it — including yourself
- in browsing through the master copy you (and others) can spot potential errors and omissions
- browsing will also give rise to ideas on how to improve the technical proposal
- it gives you some physical reassurance of progress.

Project diary During the early days of working on a proposal, people involved will find it easy to remember what has happened so far. They will be able to recall who they have spoken with, what deci- sions and promises were made, and who has, so far, done what. When pressure builds up, most of those involved will not be able to recall what they did two days ago, let alone what agreements had been made in the previous weeks. As the team leader you should

Table 25. Time spent on the task-based approach using two different frameworks

Simple, free-text approach (time spent, %)		Suggested tasks modules approach (time spent, %)	
Free text	100	Free text	20
		Tasks	40
		Modules	– (ready-prepared)

keep a project diary, and use it to record (briefly) the main events of each day. Later, when the proposal documents have been sent off, the diary will

(*a*)   help identify and allocate costs
(*b*)   help identify what went right and what went wrong — so that the next proposal will be better (in this sense it provides an input to the proposal follow-up stage, see chapter 11).

Contacts address file   Surely engineers keep a contact address file for each project, without having to be told to? The answer is not necessarily, and those that do often keep the information to themselves. Every member of the core team should have access to the same contact information, and not just the team leader.

Paper and computer files   Everyone has his own way of storing paper and computer files. It will help you if the core team agree on just one way, at least for the proposal you happen to be working on at the time. You will also probably need to keep a separate file (and computer directory) for the CVs. Their number tends to grow with time, and different versions gradually appear for each selected key staff. One example of a computer file system has separate sub-directories for

- general: general correspondence files
- maintext: main text files
- graphics: main graphics and chart files
- cost: cost proposal files (all)
- dump: for files which you may later regret having deleted
- CVs: for the CVs of selected staff
- E-mailout: for files you send out
- E-mailin: for files you receive (and keep till the proposals have been submitted)

although with the newer operating systems such as Windows 95/Windows NT, one directory per proposal would be adequate.

Style notes

Clear presentation alone will not win any project, but poor presentation can lose them. The official evaluation system awards perhaps only 2% of the points to quality of presentation (Table 19). Unofficially, the reviewer will award more points to other areas of the evaluation system, either because the documents make a good first impression, or because he can actually find the information he is looking for without any trouble. As Table 26 suggests, if the content

Table 26. Presentation and content*

	Poor presentation	Good presentation
Poor content	0	0
Good content	80	100

* % points awarded.

of the proposal is poor, even the best presentation will not save it. Where the technical content of two proposals are equally sound, the better-presented one will always win.

The style notes which you should consider include the following points.

Page layout style Preferably A4 size pages (in Europe; the USA has its own strange set of standard paper sizes). The left-hand margin should be wide enough so that you don't punch holes in the text when you are binding the document. Page headers and footers should contain information to remind the client whose proposal he is reading and what point he has reached in it; for example

- client name
- consultant or joint venture group name
- project number and title
- page number.

The page numbering should start again with each chapter or section of the document (e.g. 6.1, 6.2, . . . 6.14, then 7.1, 7.2 . . .). In this way, writing an extra page of text in one chapter will not mean having to reprint the whole document. Chapter-based page numbering also makes it a little easier when you want to prepare some sections from pre-built modules.

Page orientation You can choose to print text on an A4 page with the page oriented in either portrait (longer side vertical) or landscape (longer side horizontal) layout. Portrait is to be preferred, but in either case you should not use a mixture of the two. Readers can find it annoying if they have to keep turning a document around through 90 degrees.

Text style Use your company's own house style if it has one, since that will maintain your firm's corporate image. It also means that someone has already made the decision for you. Otherwise

- font size depends on font style (for example, Arial 11 point or 12 point is about right for most documents)

- the text style for chapter and section headings depends on their importance; don't use small, insignificant fonts for chapter headings and large, brightly-coloured fonts for unimportant sub-headings
- you should keep to one text style in the technical proposal, financial proposal and cover letters (and preferably use the same style in all your proposals)
- write the technical text in a direct, clear and concise style (for example, use active rather than passive tenses, and don't use two long words when one short one will do). The *Economist* style guide is a good reference on how to do this. If you can't write text like this, either learn, or find someone who can.
- don't be sycophantic; a phrase thanking 'the client's representative for his great help and understanding of the project shown to us during our site visit discussions' will seem overblown, especially when the representative knows he actually only spent two minutes with you talking about the weather. This text style also suggests your company is desperate to win the project.

Use of colour Colour can brighten up a technical document; overuse of it can make it look garish and cheap, and needlessly increase production costs. Also, some TOR frown on the use of colour as a frivolous distraction. Generally

- consider colour for the document cover, location plan and the main charts and graphics (the work programme and staffing schedule, for example)
- avoid the use colour on text pages.

Use of brochures Generally, you should not use brochures in technical proposals; the client will have seen the information before, either from the company representative or from the PQ document. Most brochures contain meaningless general text and add nothing of relevance to any particular proposal. Including company brochures in a technical proposal is at best a waste of money; in some cases the TOR specifically instruct consultants *not* to include them.

Number of pages In proposals, as in many other areas, quantity does not mean quality. You and your core team are not trying to create the engineering equivalent of *War and Peace*, nor do the reviewers want to read anything of the size. Some TOR limit the size of the core part of the technical proposal to 50 pages; for example the number of pages covering (*general approach, work plan and comments on the TOR*) should be limited to 50.[37]

You should consider applying this as a voluntary limit to your own document. Of course, if you aim to please your company management rather than the client, and your management is impressed by quantity, add as much irrelevant material as you like.

Other style notes

- Binders-you will find it easier to use lever-arch type binders for the technical proposal documents: you and the other members of the core team will be making changes to text and graphics up to the last minute.
- Indexed divider sheets (those with numbered tabs, where the tab number matches the document chapter number)-will help make sure that the core parts of the document are easy to find.

Technical proposal structure and contents

The technical proposal must provide the material the client asks for in the TOR, and in the order in which he wants it presented. A statement on the lines of

Provision of the requested information, in full, must be set forth *in the following sequence*[38]

(emphasis in the original) does not leave much room for argument. Nevertheless, it is always possible to provide additional, relevant material. Providing irrelevant material will simply offend the client.

The technical proposal can have as many as 16 sections. These can be sorted into three groups, which may be called (avoiding complex phraseology): **the beginning**, **the core part** of the proposal, and **the end**, as in the following summary

---

37 TOR for an ADB technical assistance project.

38 TOR for an ADB financially supported project.

- the beginning
  - section 1. title page, edge page
  - section 2. submission letter
  - section 3. table of contents
  - section 4. introduction

- the core part
  - section 5. company description and experience
  - section 6. site appreciation
  - section 7. project appreciation
  - section 8. approach and methodology (1) — task lists
  - section 9. approach and methodology (2) — technical notes
  - section 10. approach and methodology (3) — key themes
  - section 11. work programme
  - section 12. comments on the TOR
  - section 13. staff CVs

- the end
  - section 14. association agreements
  - section 15. estimates of local facilities
  - section 16. appendices/other material.

As the above suggests, the beginning explains the purpose and contents of the document; the core parts are those which receive all the formal evaluation points; and the end is a storage area for general information which does not easily fit into the other two parts.

You should try and keep the core sections together, if for no other reason than to make life easier for the reviewer. Table 27 gives an overview of what each section of the technical proposal should contain.

Table 27.   Structure and content of the technical proposal

Main section	Typical contents	
1. Title page, edge page	Title page, edge page	
2. Submission letter	Statement of intent	Contact names and details
3. Table of contents	Table of contents	List of figures
	List of tables	
4. Introduction	Structure of the document	Executive summary
	Introduction to the company(s)	Location plan
5. Company description and experience *including sub-consultants*	Description of the company(s)	Company regional experience
	Company organisation	Company current work load
	Company experience	Company backstopping ability
	Company project references	
6. Site appreciation	Site photographs	
	Client technical meetings	
7. Project appreciation	Master schedule/master plan	
	Project objectives	
8. Approach and methodology (1) task lists	Task lists	
9. Approach and methodology (2) technical notes	Approach and methodology	Optional services
	Alternative concepts	Project management methods
	Additional services	Task list
10. Approach and methodology (3) key themes	Environmental monitoring	Training/technology transfer notes
	Resettlement monitoring	Computer hardware and software
	Project management	Backstopping methods/ means
	Support for minorities	Quality Assurance
11. Work programme	Organisation chart	Staffing schedules
	Critical path chart	Man — month estimates
	Work programme	Key personnel tasks
12. Comments on the TOR		
13. Staff CVs	List of key personnel	Backstopping CV
	Key personnel CVs	List of technical support staff
	Signatures for the CVs	CVs summary table
14. Association arrangements	Association agreements	Signed copy of other documents
	Initialled copy of the TOR	
15. Estimates of local facilities	Local staff	Local accommodation
	Local transport	Local equipment
16. Appendices/other material	Site visit photographs	= possibly useful
	Company brochures	= not recommended
	List of abbreviations	= often useful
	List of definitions	= sometimes useful

The main sections of the technical proposal

The following pages discuss each of the different parts of the technical proposal in turn. They are structured in the following way.

Description

These notes show how each particular part of the proposal fits in with the rest of the document, and how much priority you should give to it, either in terms of content, or in terms of the order in which it should be completed.

Purpose of this section

Short sentences which remind you what this part of the document is supposed to show.

Priority

★★★★	1	Notes which suggest whether this part of the document
		is something which should be done straight away, and
★★★	2	preferably should have been finished yesterday
		(priority 1), or whether it can be left until the last moment
★★	3	(priority 4).
★	4	

Resources

The notes suggest which *people* and how much *time* you will need to complete this part of the technical proposal.

Links to other sections

The list shows the main links between this part of the document and the other parts and chapters.

Discussion

Discuss the contents of this part of the document, some of the problems you can expect to face in preparing it, and some ways of avoiding the problems.

Summary

Points to remember when you begin to work on this part of the document.

Section 1. Title page

Description

Purpose of this section

- Tells the client which proposal he is about to read.

Priority

★ The title page should contain colour, and so may take a little longer to print than normal text pages.

Resources

People: graphics support
Time: negligible

Links to other sections

14. Association agreements (if the title page is to list the names of the partner companies).

Discussion

The title page (and, if you are using a hardback lever arch type file, the edge page) is the first part of the document which the client will see, and so its planning is worth taking some time over.

It is also the first thing the reviewer sees when he is trying to pick one proposal from the pile of submissions he has in his office, and so should contain essential information about its contents, such as

- client logo
- project title (preferably the same title as the client used in the TOR)
- client's project reference number (also usually referred to in the TOR)
- a key colour picture or graphic (such as a location plan, or a photograph from the site visit)
- name of the JV group submitting the proposal
- names of the JV members
- document name (i.e. technical or financial proposal).

The title page is one example of the use of modules. Using the same layout for all proposal documents will save you time and give your documents a corporate image.

Summary

- The title page should be in colour.
- It should contain essential information about the contents of the document.
- Use the same layout for the title pages of the technical and financial proposals.

Section 2.   Submission letter

Description

Purpose of this section

- To tell the client which companies have prepared the proposal.
- To advise the client which persons he should contact within the consultant's organisation.
- To act as a record of the date the proposal was prepared.
- To note the main selling points of your submission.

Priority

★ The cover letter will probably need the signature of someone from the consultant's senior management; it will not take long to prepare — unless someone decides to use it as a combination of cover letter and executive summary (see below and section 4).

Resources

People: proposals team leader, company management
Time: negligible

Links to other sections

14. Association agreements (if the submission letter is to list the names of the partner companies).

Discussion

Some consultants use the submission letter as a place to write an executive summary — a brief statement of the main points of the full technical proposal. Probably the better idea is to use the submission letter as exactly that: a short letter accompanying the proposal document and telling the receiver what the document is and who it is from. The executive summary could either be provided as a section of its own, as part of the introduction to the document or, even, not be provided at all.

During your work on the technical proposal you and your colleagues may identify two or three *key themes* which you believe will make your submission stand out from all the others. They might include provision of special skills for environmental monitoring, the use of new pavement-management techniques, or the depth of the JV companies' local experience. You may have decided yourselves that these areas are worth emphasising, or the client might have expressly said they were, in the TOR. You should refer to these main selling points of your proposal, in the cover letter.

The submission letter should be no more than one page long (so that the reader can see the contact names and details straight away) and include

- project title
- client's project reference number
- name of the consultant or JV group submitting the proposal
- names of the JV members
- document name (i.e. technical or financial proposal)
- consultant's contact name and details
- signature of someone from the company management.

Summary

- Leave time to collect the appropriate signatures.

Section 3. Table of contents

Description

Purpose of this section

- To give the reviewer an overview of the structure and contents of the document.
- To give the proposals team an overview of the structure and contents of the document.
- To show the client where to find individual charts, CVs, text etc.

Priority

★★★ Prepare a rough draft at the start of work on the technical proposal.

★ The final version of the table of contents has to wait until all the other sections are ready.

Resources

People: team leader, general support
Time: negligible *to* 1 day (allowing for QA checks)

Links to other sections

1–16. By definition, the table of contents has links to all the other sections of the document.

Discussion

The table of contents is a useful place to store more than just chapter headings and page numbers. It should also tell the reader where to find the important charts and tables — task lists, table of key personnel, work programmes and staffing schedules, for example. The table of contents should also contain an explanation of those words and abbreviations in the main document, with which most readers will not be familiar.

The table of contents itself should contain no more than three heading levels; more than this and it becomes so detailed that it loses its value as an overview of the document.

The section should contain the following

- table of contents
- list of tables
- list of figures and charts
- list of abbreviations
- list of definitions.

Summary

- It's a good idea to keep a working table of contents from the start of work on the document — it can help the proposals team as much as the reviewers.
- Any document more than 2–3 pages long should have a table of contents.

Section 4. Introduction

Description

Purpose of this section

- To introduce the client to the structure and contents of the document.
- To introduce the client to the company or companies who are submitting the proposal.
- To describe the relationship between these companies.
- To summarise the background to the proposal.
- To list the relevant background documents.

Priority

★ The final version of the introduction has to wait until the final version of the table of contents is ready, the tasks of each member company have been defined, and the client has no further opportunity to issue amendments to the TOR.

Resources

People: team leader, general support
Time: negligible

Links to other sections

3. Table of contents
5. Company description

Discussion

General

The introduction should be just that: it introduces the member companies who are submitting the proposal, and introduces the proposal document. It tells the client

(*a*)   who you are
(*b*)   where you come from
(*c*)   where you are going to take him.

The *who* lists the member companies and explains what they can offer for this particular project. For example, one might be a specialist in rural development policy, another in the supervision of construction projects, while a third might be the local partner. This part should also indicate which company is the lead member, and which are sub-consultants (and so outside the joint venture group). It may also refer to individual freelancers, particularly if they have an international reputation. You should keep these company notes very brief as the client already knows who you are, or else he wouldn't have selected your company for the short list, and there is plenty of scope for describing the companies in detail under section 5, Company description.

Where you come from describes the history of the events leading up to the proposal, and lists the various documents which either form part of the TOR, which the client later sent as amendments or extensions to the TOR, or which give further information on the project (and which you were lucky enough to obtain by other means). Examples of the last group would be a copy of the feasibility study (if the new project is to carry out a detailed road design), of the Environmental Impact Assessment, and of the local highway design standards. These notes not only helps the general reader but also, later on, they will serve as reminders for you and other people in your company, and explain how you came to be involved in the proposal in the first place.

Where you are going to take the client allows you to remind him of the headings and contents of the following main chapters of the document. If you have used a task-based approach to preparing the proposal it can help to point it out now; and if you have identified some main themes, now is the time to tell the client where in the document you discuss them.

Executive summary

Very often, a long technical report will contain an executive summary. These are short (perhaps two to four pages) free-standing documents, and are meant for the busy reader who is mainly interested in reading the report's conclusions and recommendations, rather than how the consultant arrived at them.

So far as technical proposals are concerned, an executive summary could remind the reviewer of the key features of your proposal offer, and of any special services you want to emphasise. If translated into the language of the client's home country, they can also inform and influence non English-speakers in his organisation. Executive summaries place an extra burden on the proposals team (especially if they have to be translated), since they can normally only be prepared at the last minute, when the proposals team is already under considerable time pressure.

Having said this, an executive summary gives you the chance to restate the main selling points of your proposal, and in the one place which anyone who handles your proposal will feel obliged to read.

Location plan

Many international projects involve locations which the normal reader would not be familiar with, and names which can be difficult to remember. A location plan is a helpful key graphic that the general reader (and the document writer) can refer back to.

Summary

- Keep the company descriptions brief.
- Accept the pain of preparing an executive summary.

Section 5. Company description

Description

Purpose of this section

- To show the client that the consulting companies have an established business presence.
- To show that the consulting companies have appropriate *regional* experience.
- To show that the consulting companies have appropriate *sector* experience.

Priority

★★ Not particularly urgent, but it helps to do it early, and get it out of the way.

Resources

People: team leader, technical experts, general support, graphics support

Time: 1–2 weeks, depending on how many companies are involved, what countries they are in, whether you are using modules, and whether you want to include colour pages

Links to other sections

8. Approach and methodology (1) — task lists
9. Approach and methodology (2) — technical notes
10. Approach and methodology (3) — special services
14. Association arrangements

Discussion

The company description covers two parts: the business background of the company, and its relevant experience in carrying out the same type of project in similar parts of the world. Part of the core of the technical proposal, it scores some 10% of the evaluation points. This still means that you have to take care in preparing it. In close international competition, less than 5% points can separate the winning proposal from the runner-up.

Your company should have a pool of text, tables and graphics documents which describe itself and the projects it has worked on. Even better, you should use databases. These will allow you to produce a proposal-specific set of project references with the minimum time and effort.

Life may not be so simple if you are working with other companies as part of a joint venture. They may not have any suitable material at all — perhaps because what they have doesn't match the layout which the TOR call for, or because most or their material is prepared in their home language (i.e. not English). There is also the risk that these companies are based in another continent; whatever the quality of their material, it can still take them weeks to send it to you (not everyone is using the Internet). Your team will also need time to collate the documents, probably changing the computer files or retyping the information to a standard page layout (e.g. font, headers, footers). It's safe to assume that problems will crop up. You should *not* leave the preparation of this section until the last minute.

Material on business background

Different TOR ask for different information on the consulting companies submitting the proposal. The first step in selecting what details to give about your company is to re-read the TOR, find out what they are asking for, and answer the question. You may decide to provide more detail than requested, but it should be relevant detail: long, padded business notes can both bore and annoy the reviewer. They will also suggest you have not understood the TOR. The information you may be asked (or decide) to provide may include the following

- *company history*: clients do not necessarily believe that a long-established company is more likely to do better work than a recently created one, but it may suggest that the older company is less likely to go bust during the course of the project
- *business structure*: clients are cautious about the possible conflict of interest that may occur when consultants are owned by contracting companies[39] or other organisations which may be related to the project (local quangos for example)

---

39 For example, ADB *Guidelines on the use of consultants by the ADB and its borrowers*, para. 5.04, on engineering firms related to contractors or manufacturers. 1996 reprint.

- *organisation*: companies with offices in the project region are likely to have more local knowledge and a better understanding of the area's cultural and engineering difficulties
- *current activities*: this information can show that the consultants are still active in the type of work which the new project will involve, and that they have the spare resources to carry it out
- *current key staff*: a list of key staff can show that the consultant still has the appropriate skills which the project calls for (project references show that the company had the necessary skills in the past; they do not necessarily show that it has them in the present)
- *key themes*: the TOR won't mention these, but you may have identified them as the main selling points of your proposal. It is worth pointing out that you have the resources and the organisation to provide excellent service in these subjects.

Material on relevant experience

There are two types of relevant experience: experience your company has of working in the project *region*, and the experience it has of working in the technical *sectors* covered by the new project. You can demonstrate both types of experience by using project references, i.e. notes on individual projects which your company either carried out in the past, or is working on now. Project references come in several forms (see chapter 12) and may contain any combination of text, tables and graphics. You should select the project references according to the following

- *what the TOR ask for*: the TOR will often specify the number, layout and age of the project references, e.g. 'projects . . . completed within the last 10 years . . .'[40]
- *relevance*: if the project is for the maintenance of rural feeder roads in Sri Lanka, then you will not win any points by describing the motorway interchanges you have designed in Britain. If your company doesn't have any relevant project references, then perhaps it should not be submitting a proposal for the new project.

---

40 TOR for an ADB technical assistance project.

- *key themes*: again, these are the main selling points of your proposal, and you should select project references to show that your company has experience in the technical sectors which they cover.

Layout of the section

Once again there are two different points to consider here: the order of the different parts of the section, and the design of the parts themselves. Generally, you should provide the information in the order, and using the forms, which the TOR specify. Otherwise, Table 28 shows one possible structure. The table suggests that the notes on business background come first, grouped by company. Project references should follow, grouped first by type and subject of project reference (long, short, regional or sector experience), and only secondly by company.

The question of whether the notes should be include text, tables or graphics depends on what the TOR ask for, what the client will accept, and what you have already prepared (in your modules). Some clients object to the inclusion of colour graphics, which they may see as unnecessary padding. It may be easier to have the notes on business background in text, the notes on relevant experience in the form of tables, and collate colour material and graphics at the end of the section. It is also worth remembering that

- keeping text together makes for easier reading
- keeping tables together makes for an easier overview
- keeping graphics together makes for easier duplication and collating.

Table 28. One possible structure for company description

Main heading	Sub-heading
Business background	
Company (1)	History
Company (2)	Business structure
etc.	Organisation
	Current activities
	Current key staff
Relevant experience	
Regional	Company (1)
Sector	Company (2)
	etc.

Notes. The questions which this section is trying to answer are
(*a*) who are the companies? (so sort the notes on business background by companies first), and
(*b*) what experience does the JV have? (so sort by type of experience first).

Summary

- Read the TOR (again) before starting work on this section.
- Answer the question.
- Choose the project references to match the regional and sector experience required.
- Keep to a simple structure for the section.
- Avoid the use of irrelevant (padding) material.
- Use project references for schemes carried out by your company, and not for schemes carried out by your current employees when they were working for someone else.

Section 6. Site appreciation

Description

Purpose of this section

- To give the reader an idea of the physical nature of the project site.
- To provide background to the selected project approach and methodology.

Priority

★★★★ The proposals team experts will have difficulty in proposing the most suitable techniques if they have no idea what the project site looks like.

Resources

People: local partner, country expert
Time: 1–2 days (much of the material should come from the site visit)

Links to other sections

7. Project appreciation
9. Approach and methodology (2) — technical notes

Discussion

Every country has regions with unique microclimates or micro-geography. The UK, for example, has the Lake District and Dartmoor, London's Oxford Street and Portsmouth's Commercial Road. It can be difficult for someone who has not visited these places to understand their particular characteristics, and so to select the appropriate methodology to use for a new project there.

The site visit should produce a useful set of photographs, and technical notes describing some of the area's particular, project-related peculiarities. One source for these notes should be the meetings with the client and the local partner.

Summary

- Make sure the site visit produces some suitable photographs.

Section 7. Project appreciation

Description

Purpose of this section

- To give an idea of how the project fits into the client's overall development programme (and so to explain some of the time constraints which operate on it).
- To explain the aims and objectives which the project is meant to work to.
- To provide further background to the selected project approach and methodology.

Priority

★★★★ The proposals team will be better able to define suitable tasks and work programme if they have an understanding of the external constraints and objectives.

Resources

People: proposals team leader, local partner, country expert
Time: 1–2 days (much of the material should come from the site visit)

Links to other sections

6. Site appreciation
8. Approach and methodology (1) — task list
9. Approach and methodology (2) — technical notes

Discussion

Most projects are just one more step in a larger, overall development programme. For example, a potential client wants to build a new road for more reasons than he likes to see several kilometres of freshly-laid asphalt. The road is part of an overall network development programme and has to be finished

(*a*) at the same time as the new river bridge is completed, or
(*b*) before construction of a new industrial district can begin in town.

Research from the site visit and interviews should provide you with current information on the background to the project. The freshest information should come from your local partner and your company's regional or country office.

Summary

- Identify external constraints.
- Understand the client's aims and objectives.

Section 8.   Approach and methodology (1) — task lists

Description

Purpose of this section

- To create the structure around which to build the rest of the document.
- To show the client that the tasks he has specified are the tasks you propose to carry out.
- To help in the allocation of tasks between companies and between the key personnel.

Priority

★★★★ Top priority — until you know what you are supposed to be doing, you cannot describe how, with whom (and for how much) you will carry it out.

Resources

People: team leader, technical experts, country expert
Time: 1–2 days, with amendments and revisions developing later

Links to other sections

1–16. (all)

Discussion

Tasks are the main steps in the process you would follow to carry out the services required by the new project. They are a familiar idea to anyone who has worked with project management software, and to anyone who has written a user manual. With a little thought you could probably define two or three hundred tasks for the project your company is interested in, but you would be making a rod for your own back[41], and probably confuse the client into the bargain. For a

---

41   Each task needs some explanation in the technical notes, the work programme and staffing schedules.

Table 29. Example of a structured task list

Work area	Main task	Sub-task	TOR para
Specified tasks			
Collect background data	Carry out traffic surveys	Peak hour classified count	6.1(a)
		Daily volume count	6.1(b)
	Make land-use surveys	Estimate gross floor area (GFA) by type	7
		Survey shopper group size	9.2
Forecast future traffic			
Carry out route assignment			
Additional tasks			
Optional tasks			

Notes. The first two columns would appear in the task list; the third column would only appear in the technical notes (next section).

major bid, then perhaps 60–100 tasks would be needed. The task list itself should be linked to a one to two-page summary table (and, preferably, one page). Here the tasks may be grouped either in terms of main tasks and sub-tasks (see Table 29) or in terms of project phases and tasks.

In some cases it is important to explain which company is responsible for which tasks. For example, the TOR may note that

> In cases involving a collaboration arrangement between a consulting firm . . . and domestic consultants . . . *the services to be provided by the domestic consultants . . . should be clearly defined and set forth in the proposals and in the contract.*[42] (own emphasis)

Types of task

There are three types of task: those which the TOR specify, additional tasks and optional tasks. The first type is self-explanatory. For the other two, perhaps the writer of the TOR omitted to mention some tasks, or perhaps you and your colleagues simply have some new ideas. In both cases they are tasks which the TOR does not

42 ADB *Guidelines on the use of consultants by the ADB and its borrowers,* para 4.03.(c), 1996 reprint.

mention. The main difference between them is that additional tasks are important (even essential) to the project, while optional tasks are not. In other words, you definitely propose to carry out the additional tasks, but only suggest the optional tasks (and would need additional fees and resources to do so). For example,

- *specified task*: supervise the reconstruction of 100 km of local feeder road
- *additional task*: prepare a five-year maintenance programme for the reconstructed road
- *optional task*: produce a GIS-based vector plan of the completed road, with a backdrop raster image of the surrounding countryside.

There is a fourth type of task: unnecessary tasks. These are ones which you should take care to avoid, since they will increase the cost of your proposal but will not add anything extra to the project. An example might be

- *unnecessary task*: proposing speed surveys on a rural feeder road.

You should consider including the specified and additional tasks in the normal work programme and staffing schedules, and include the optional tasks under a separate item in the financial proposal.

Structured task list

The task list should be a table, with each task described in no more than 10–15 words (this simplifies the preparation of work programme charts etc.). It helps if you can give the tasks a structure of their own, for example

- *work areas*: groupings of similar or related tasks
- *main tasks*: the main steps in carrying out the work, and would appear in the detailed work programme
- *sub-tasks*: related, minor activities, and would not appear in the detailed work programme.

The task list could include a column giving the paragraph reference where it is referred to in the TOR, and the description of each task should use the same words as the TOR. These points make it easier for the reviewer to check off the tasks in the TOR with the tasks you describe in your proposal.

Summary

- Prepare the task list as a top priority.
- Relate the task list to the TOR.
- Don't get carried away with enthusiasm and specify more services than are sensibly needed.
- Keep the task list to one page.
- Keep the description of each task to 10–15 words.
- Give the tasks some sort of structure.
- Try and include one or two optional tasks — they show you have innovative ideas.

Section 9. Approach and methodology (2) — technical notes

Description

Purpose of this section

- To describe what technical methods you would use to implement the tasks in the task list.
- To explain why you chose these methods.
- To discuss the technical problems which the project could involve.

Priority

★★★ Not as urgent as the work programme and task lists, working on the technical notes can suggest new ideas for both these areas, and should follow close on their heels.

Resources

People: technical writer, country expert, technical experts
Time: 2 weeks (at least)

Links to other sections

  5. Company description
  8. Approach and methodology (1) — task lists
 11. Work programme
 13. Staff CVs

Discussion

This section is part of the core of the technical proposal, and may even seem the most important part of it. It isn't. More points will be awarded to the section which includes the work programme and staffing schedule, and many more points will be awarded to the staff CVs. Nevertheless, the client is looking to employ international engineering consultants, and so he will expect this section to be technically *correct* and *relevant* to his region and his project. This is why the technical and country experts should work together in preparing them.

Where different companies or even different people are preparing the notes, time may become a problem. One cause is the difficulty of actually collecting the material in one place, another is the style of the material collated. The notes should read as if they were written by one person in one office. Creating this impression may mean that the technical writer has to substantially redraft other people's work.

Contents

Preparing the notes for this section should be easy, if your proposals team has the right mix. The task list tells them what to write about, and the technical and country experts will decide together what to write. You should remind your colleagues that it is not enough to write a general statement about each task. The notes should contain the following elements

- *basic task*: for example, the design of a new rural feeder road
- *technical content*: the approach you propose to use
- *local content*: the local design standards, the local problems affecting the design (such as animal-drawn traffic or cycles, roadside street traders, villages which the road will pass through)
- *local knowledge*: reference to the local authorities who may be involved in approving the design, knowledge of the client's organisation, of the project history (why is the road needed, is it likely to be widened or upgraded in the future, has the land been acquired).

This is where the information from the site appreciation and project appreciation becomes extremely useful.

Other notes

This section can win few points, but it can lose a lot more, if you and your team underestimate the client and his reviewers. At least one consultant has been known to base his technical notes on copying directly from a reference work (which the reviewer had also read). Another included a layout plan where the draughtsman had mistakenly used local religious symbols for non-religious buildings. The client rejected the proposal because of its lack of sensitivity and local knowledge.

Summary

- Prepare technically sound material — at least one of the reviewers will be an expert in the type of work covered by the new project.
- Be careful of using modules for this section: good technical notes are based on *local* knowledge and *local* problems.
- Don't quote parrot-fashion from textbooks — the reviewer probably read them before you did.
- Find and use someone who can write readable text.

Section 10. Approach and methodology (3) — key themes

Description

Purpose of this section

- To emphasise those services in the proposal which you believe are particularly important.
- To emphasise those services in the proposal which the client believes are particularly important.

Priority

★★★ As with the technical notes, working on the key themes can suggest new ideas for the task list and work programme.

Resources

People: technical writer, country expert, technical experts
Time: 2 weeks (at least)

Links to other sections

- 5. Company description
- 8. Approach and methodology (1) — task lists
- 11. Work programme
- 13. Staff CVs

Discussion

Some of the services you propose will be particularly important to the client or to the funding agency — and sometimes, even to both. The TOR may mention them specifically, they may be a regular theme in the funding agency's publications, or the client may have stressed them during meetings arranged as part of the site visit. Whatever the source of interest, the reviewer is likely to find them important and he would expect the consultant to write some appropriate text on them. He would also like to be able to find the text easily, which is one reason for putting it in a separate section or sub-section of the document. Typical quotes on key themes include *support for minorities*: consideration of vulnerable groups is regarded by the Bank as an important means to improve project quality and implementation[43]

quality assurance: the main objective of the consultancy services is to ensure that the highest possible construction quality is achieved[44]

technology transfer: foreign consultants should select people who can communicate effectively and harmoniously, preferably with a knowledge of the local language or a willingness to learn[45]

Possible key themes

Many of the key themes occur again and again. You and your technical experts should be able to prepare standard modules for many of them in advance of any work on proposals. Frequent key themes include

- backstopping
- computer hardware/ software
- environmental monitoring/ environmental protection
- project management
- quality assurance

- resettlement monitoring
- support for minorities
- technology transfer
- stakeholder involvement
- cost effectiveness/ value for money.

Summary

- Find out what the key selling points of your proposal are, and emphasise them.
- Prepare standard notes on key themes when you are not in the middle of a crisis (which is the situation most proposals develop into).

---

43 ADB Annual Report 1995, page 74.

44 TOR for an ADB financially supported project.

45 FIDIC *Guidelines on quality-based selection of consulting engineers, page 15, 1991.*

Section 11. Work programme

Description

Purpose

- To prove that the resources you propose to use can complete the project within the time allowed.
- To show how you propose to organise the project team.
- To show how would carry out liaison and coordination activities.
- To show the project management structure of the project team.
- To demonstrate how you arrive at the total resources you need for the project.
- To provide part of the base information for the financial proposal.

Priority

★★★★ The work programme confirms (or otherwise) the first ideas on the size and composition of the project team, and produces the basic input to the financial proposal; you should start on it as soon as you have prepared the task list.

Resources

People: team leader, project management expert, technical expert, graphics support

Time: 1–2 weeks, allowing for revisions

Links to other sections

8. Approach and methodology (1) — task lists
9. Approach and methodology (2) — technical notes
10. Approach and methodology (3) — key themes
12. Comments on the TOR
13. Staff CVs

Discussion

Need for accuracy

This is the section where you get down to business. The client wants someone to carry out a project; you have to prove to him that your project team can do it, technically, on time and within budget. If the project team consists of two people on a single, six-month assignment, then this section will be very easy. For more complicated projects, developing the various elements of the work programme *must* take some time. Inaccurate results risk your company losing the project; they even risk your winning the project, and then losing your company money (which is even worse). Points to look out for

- *inconsistency*: the reviewer notices some contradictions between the work programme and the staffing schedule; this suggests to him that, since your company cannot prepare a sensible management programme for the proposal, then it certainly won't be able to manage the project (it can also suggest that your company is not taking the client and his project seriously).
- *poor programming*: an implausible programme will leave the site staff with an impossible job; and you cannot argue that 'the site team can put things right', or 'a better programme can be produced during contract negotiations'. The site team can only work with the resources your programme allows for; and some TOR state that the work programme submitted in the proposal is legally binding. Of course, if the project does go wrong because of the programme, the proposals team can always blame the project team.
- *poor resourcing*: the work programme includes the preparation of a staffing schedule, which shows the assignment (months and number of visits) of key personnel. The staffing schedule provides the basic information for the financial proposal. If the work programme which you prepare proves to be impracticable then the assignments may have to be increased. Your company will probably have to bear the extra costs, and may end up by losing a lot of money on the project.

Techniques

For more than the most straight-forward of projects you should work with project management software. As the proposals team work on the documents they will continue to revise their ideas. This will lead to changes in the different elements of the work programme. You will find it both easier and more reliable to make these changes by computer, rather than by hand. Certainly, manually-prepared charts can be more attractive than those which most project management programmes can produce, but you need accuracy more than artistic beauty.

In most proposals, the work programme covers very much the same elements. Once you have developed a reliable package for one proposal, you will be able to use it as a module for most of the later ones your company works on; so spending a little time to get it right at the beginning can save you and your company a lot of time later on.

The reviewer will more easily understand your proposals for the various elements of the work programme if you present them in the form of tables and graphics; usually the TOR insist that you do so, and give you examples of the layouts which you should use. You will still need to write some text to introduce the tables, and to explain points such as deviations from the TOR.

Elements of the work programme

There are some eleven elements that make up the work programme activities (Fig 10). Although the TOR may not ask you to show all eleven of them in the proposal, you will probably need to consider them

- *task list*: the primary input to the work programme, and a separate section of the technical proposal.
- *task sheets*: the raw material which the consultant provides (and the client pays for), is people. The task sheets provide the first links between the project tasks to the project staff — between *what* has to be done and *who* will do it. They also describe the sequence of the various tasks. For example, the task sheets take input *from* the task list and provide output *to* the work programme (Fig. 11).
- *key personnel tasks*: once you know what has to be done and who has to do it, you can select the key personnel. These, the senior local or foreign experts in the project team, must have the appropriate qualifications and experience to carry out the tasks assigned to them. You will not win a proposal by selecting staff at random and improving their CVs later on (see section 13).
- *CVs*: the curriculum vitae of the key personnel (biodata is an alternative name): also a separate part of the technical proposal.
- *work programme*: a time-based diagram or chart showing the tasks and the sequence you propose to carry out the tasks in, and indicating the main phases and events of the work. Examples would be

- data collection
- design review
- construction supervision

- submission of design review report
- submission of existing situation report
- submission of final handover report.

- *staffing schedule*: a time-based diagram or chart showing the periods when the key personnel will be actively working on the project, either on site or from their home office. The staffing schedule must be consistent with the work programme — key personnel have to be available when the work programme shows their tasks are to take place.
- *organisation chart*: it's not enough to have 20 people busy working on site — someone has to be in charge, someone has to coordinate with the client's representatives and with the consultant's home office. The organisation chart

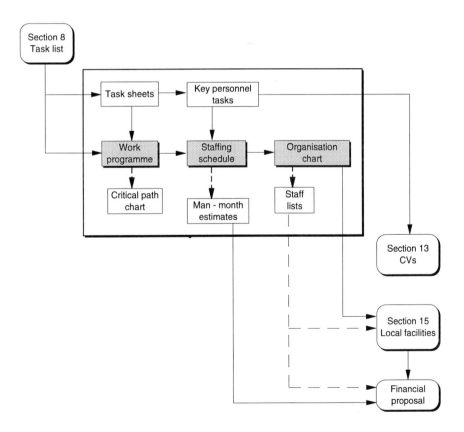

Fig. 10. Elements in the work programme

Description of variant	Staffing schedule				Assignment		
	Month				Total months		Return
	6	12	18	24	Field	Home	tickets
1. Site staff expected to work for two years without a break					24	0	1
2. Site staff allowed reasonable periods of leave; no replacement					22	0	2
3. Site staff allowed reasonable leave periods, consultant provides a temporary replacement					25*	0	3

* Includes two, two-week travel and handover periods

Assumptions

Leave allowance	=	2 months a year
Salary	=	US$ 3000 per month
Assignment	=	2 years
Staff contracts	=	Allow 1 return ticket each 12 months
Leave tickets	=	Cost US$ 2000
Per diem	=	(30 day month* at US$ 20) = US$ 600

Fig. 11. *Core team staffing schedule — variations*

Table 30. *Total months of service (work and leave)*

Variant	Permanent staff		Replacement			%min	
	Work	Leave	Work	Leave	Total	Time	Tickets
1	24	4·8	–	–	28·8	1·09	1
2	22	4·4	–	–	26·4	1·00	2
3	22	4·4	3	0·6	30	1·14	3

Note. Costs to consultant — he has to pay the least staff costs in varient 2.

Table 31. *Costs to client (US$ thousand)*

Variant	Remuneration	Per diem	Tickets	Total	%min
1	72	14·4	2	88·4	1·06
2	66	13·2	4	83·2	1
3	72	14·4	6	92·4	1·11

Note. Client also has to pay the least costs in variant 2.

shows these internal and external coordination and management links.

- *critical path chart*: requested in at least one TOR, the critical path chart is a standard project management technique. It is a time-based diagram or chart, developed from the work programme, and shows which particular tasks are most likely to cause delay or disruption to the overall project.
- *man–month estimates*: a table showing the amount of time each of the key personnel will be working on the project, and whether he will be working from his home office or in the field (this affects the rates charged for his work).
- *staff lists*: the project staff will include more than just the key personnel — in most cases they will need the help of a number of technical support staff (local engineers and technicians, such as materials laboratory assistants) and non-technical support staff (ranging from secretaries to guards and drivers).
- *local facilities*: a separate section of the technical proposal, it describes the physical assets which the project team will need during their work in the project country; for example, local office space and transport for the key personnel, technical and non-technical support staff. The project organisation will also affect the estimates of local facilities (e.g. a decision to set up two site supervision teams will mean that the project will need two site offices).

The financial proposal is a completely separate document which takes as input the man–months, local facilities and support staff estimates, and produces as output the estimated total cost of the consultant's services.

Notes on the elements

The *work programme* should show the tasks, the work areas and the main events in the programme (milestones in the project management phrase). It can help to include events which you might not have identified as separate tasks, but which set the new project against the background of what else is happening in the area. Examples include

- completion of pre-project feasibility study
- project start-up period/mobilisation period
- maintenance period on completion of project (even design and feasibility studies allow some time at the end of the project for the client to ask for explanations or corrections;

and there is also usually a 12-month retention period for the final payment).

The most difficult question with the *staffing schedule* is how (or even whether) to show leave periods. Suppose the project will last two years, and you propose a full-time project manager. You can cover this in (at least) three ways.

- If the sample staffing schedule in the TOR shows a solid line for this position, perhaps you should as well (variant 1, Fig. 11). This will damage the quality of the work on the scheme, as the project manager is likely to have a nervous breakdown before the two years are up. Everyone needs a holiday from time to time, and project managers more than most.

- If you allow the project manager to take his earned, two-months leave during the 24 months of the contract (variant 2) then

  o he will only be working for 22 months (and your company will lose two months' fees)
  o he will expect you to pay for his return leave ticket
  o his post will be vacant for the two months he is away.

(Very often key personnel on longer-term overseas projects will want to take leave every six months or so; one break every eleven months understates the problem).

- You may decide to provide a temporary replacement for the project manager (variant 3). In this case, although the project will have coverage for 24 months, the client will pay for 24 months, and

  o you will have to pay for two travel and handover periods at each end of the leave period
  o there will be another return ticket to pay for.

Which way you decide to cover the question of leave periods depends partly on what the TOR allow, and what the members of the project team can reasonably expect if they are to stay on top of their work. The TOR are often quite specific. For example,

> one extra round trip will be reimbursed for every 24 months of assignment in the (project) country[46]

---

46 World Bank *Standard form of contract: consultants services — complex time-based assignments*, page 34, June 1995.

and

> leave taken during an assignment (is not an acceptable social cost) if no additional staff replacement is provided[47]

At this point the problem becomes more relevant to the financial proposal than the technical proposal. The businessman and the accountant may decide to charge the client for an additional leave period and return ticket under the heading of 'task 27: design review with head office experts'. The proposal team leader should make sure that the working conditions of the project team (including leave arrangements) are sufficient to give the team members a reasonable working environment *and* that they are covered by the financial proposal. For further details see Tables 30 and 31.

The *organisation chart* has to show both the internal and external organisation. The *internal* organisation shows the hierarchy and structure of the project team and their opposite numbers in the client's organisation. The *external* organisation shows the liaison and coordination links between the consultant and

(*a*) the senior management of the client's organisation

(*b*) the funding agency (where different)

(*c*) local authorities, service undertakers and NGOs

(*d*) other consultants working in the same area.

Summary

- The main point to remember about the work programme is that it should be

  ○ plausible
  ○ compatible (e.g. with the financial proposal)
  ○ priceable.

- However you decide to show leave periods, make sure that the technical and the financial proposals are consistent.
- If you decide to differ from the TOR, explain your reasons in the accompanying text.
- Don't over-elaborate the work programme — you are preparing it for a project proposal, and not for the project itself.
- The first staffing list is usually over-the-top. Aim to produce a final version with at least 20% less man – months.

---

47 TOR for a World Bank financed project.

Section 12.   Comments on the TOR

Description

Purpose of this Section

- To make a note of potential problems which the TOR may have overlooked.
- To point out ambiguities in the TOR.
- To summarise any additional and optional tasks you may have suggested.

Priority

★★ This section has to wait until you have finished the notes on approach and methodology and the work programme.

Resources

People: team leader
Time: negligible to 1 day

Links to other Sections

8.   Approach and methodology (1) — task lists
9.   Approach and methodology (2) — technical notes
10. Approach and methodology (3) — key themes
11. Work programme

Discussion

Consultants are supposed to be experts in their particular field of activity, and so you should not be surprised if the proposals team disagree with some parts of the TOR. If you have major problems with the TOR, then you should contact the client directly. Most will allow consultants to submit questions on the project up to two weeks before the date of submission. In the worst case, and where the client does not give a satisfactory reply, you can decline to submit a proposal. More often, the comments will only be minor. Perhaps the TOR are ambiguous, or you have a better idea. For example

- you believe the TOR suggests the wrong mix of staff
- the TOR asks for the proposal to be submitted in two

languages, but does not say which is to be the lead language
- you wish to suggest some additional or optional tasks.

In these cases, the 'comments on the TOR' is a place to summarise your ideas rather than to discuss them. For each one you list, you should indicate which part of the TOR it refers to, and where your proposal document considers it in detail. You can also use the comments as coat hooks' for points which you might want to raise during contract negotiations. The question of the lead language would be one example.

You are unlikely to win any points for flattery. Comments such as 'the TOR were exceedingly clear and well-written' would make most reviewers wonder (a) what the TOR have omitted, and (b) what the consultant is trying to hide.

Summary

- There's no need to be sycophantic.
- Don't argue.
- Keep the comments brief — any discussion notes should be put elsewhere in the text.
- With each comment, include a reference to the appropriate TOR paragraph.

Section 13.   Staff CVs

Description

Purpose of this section

- To describe the key personnel you have selected to carry out the project for the client.
- To describe the key personnel in such a way that they win the maximum points.
- To certify that the CV descriptions are correct and that the personnel will be available.

Priority

★★★★ You should begin work on the CVs straight away; even so you will probably still be working on them up to the last minute.

Resources

People: team leader, businessman, general support
Time: more than you will have available

Links to other Sections

8. Approach and methodology (1) — task lists

Discussion

The staff who the consultant proposes for the project team are important. As one source indicates

> Of the various factors (in the evaluation of proposals) the primary emphasis should be given to the personnel assigned to the work.[48]

Staff CVs are the main source of information on the key personnel. They can account for up to 60% of the evaluation points, and can

---

48   ADB *Guidelines on the use of consultants by the ADB and its borrowers*, para 6.10.(b), 1996 reprint.

win or lose the project for you. In most cases, preparing the CVs for a proposal involves three main steps

- selecting the key personnel
- preparing the CVs
- obtaining their signatures (where requested in the TOR).

Selecting the key personnel

You should have made the first attempt at this during the preparation stage, when you were deciding whether to team up with other consultants for the project. As you work on the proposal, your ideas on what staff to propose will change. Revising the task lists, for example, will mean revising the key personnel list — adding an optional task may mean that you will need to suggest an additional, optional expert. There is also the possibility that you decide to modify the task list and task sheets to provide a better match with the people you want to propose.

When you begin to work on the financial proposal you may discover other reasons for changing the selected staff. For example, the first choice of expert for a particular post may expect to take his family with him (with all the extra costs which that implies) but the second choice would be content with a bachelor-status assignment and one leave ticket every twelve months. Perhaps the person you had in mind is simply no longer available. After all, companies use the same staff in several different proposals since most have a limited number of key personnel that they can propose. Individual freelancers will also allow their details to be included in a number of proposals (although rarely for the same project). They are aware that each proposal has on average a 1 in 6 chance of success, and those are pretty low odds on which to base their next year's salary expectations.

You and your proposals team will probably have to look out for changes in the selected key personnel until almost the last minute.

Preparing the CVs

Your company probably proposes the same key staff time after time, and so you should have plenty of ready material for the CVs you need for your proposal. All that has to be done is then to change the material to match the layout for the CVs which the TOR specifies, and to check with the CVs owner

(*a*) for any useful updates
(*b*) or more detailed information on experience he has which is particularly important to this proposal.

As a starter, your company should have detailed CVs available for those of its experts who have at least ten years of professional experience, have worked overseas, and can speak English. However, since all a consultant has to sell are the services of its professional staff, you should aim for a ready supply of CVs for *all* of them.

Obtaining signatures

This may seem the simplest thing to arrange; in fact, it is often the most difficult. *Simple* when only one company is making the proposal and all its staff work from one office. *Difficult* because most international proposals are prepared by groups of companies, each of which works from a number of offices; because many of the key personnel will be on assignment in some remote corner of the world, and because clients insist on original signatures.

The clients want original signatures to reassure themselves that the selected personnel have agreed to work with the consultant on this project. They also want some assurance that what the CV says is true.

The end result is that the consultant is often faced with an impossible situation. On the one hand, he needs the original signatures at least two weeks before the submission date, to allow time for duplicating and posting the proposal documents. On the other hand, he may not have prepared the revised CVs until two weeks before the submission date. As a result, consultants will have to have obtained a written agreement from the person concerned to be included in the consultant's team.

Other points on CVs

There are various types and layouts for CVs; some CVs need to be improved, but there must be a limit between valid improvement and wild exaggeration. The whole question of CVs is worth more detailed discussion (see chapter 12).

Summary

- Submit the CVs in the form that the TOR asks you to use.
- Match what the client is looking for (the tasks) with what the person has to offer.
- Don't forget to get the signatures on the CVs.
- Keep an up-to-date list of the key personnel you are proposing.
- Have someone outside the proposals team carry out an independent evaluation of the CVs (ghost-mark them) before proceeding to the final edit.

Section 14. Association arrangements

Description

Purpose of this Section

- To show the client which companies the lead consultant proposes to carry out the work with.
- To describe how these companies intend to share the work.
- To provide documentary evidence that the companies have some sort of written agreement.
- To show compliance with the TOR (for example, where these require the lead consultant to associate with a local company).

Priority

★★★★ Your company should have decided who it wants to work with before you begin work on the technical proposal (see chapter 5).

★ Originals of the declarations of association have to be ready in time for the production of the final proposal documents.

Resources

People: businessman, team leader and company links
Time: negligible to 2 weeks, depending on how seriously you want to treat this part of the work

Links to other Sections

5. Company description and experience
13. Staff CVs

Discussion

Three Levels of Association

In many cases, companies prefer to carry out international projects in association with other firms. They may do so either through choice (perhaps to provide regional or subject strengths where they themselves are weak), or because the TOR require them to. The associations are generally one of three types. At the upper level, the companies agree to share the risks and responsibilities. They agree to carry *joint and several liability* for the work to be carried out. Such joint ventures have a lead company which makes the formal direct link with the client. At the second level, the lead company arranges the contract with the client, and recruits other consultants to provide limited specialist services through sub-contracts with itself. The sub-consultancy agreements do not imply any joint and several liability of the junior partner. At the lowest level, the lead company or the sub-consultant recruits the services of a single individual specialist. In brief

- joint ventures are agreements between equal partner companies (with one partner being more equal than the others)
- sub-consultancies are agreements between non-equal partners
- freelancer agreements are between a company and an individual.

Information to give to the client

As always, you must give the client the information he specifically asks for in the TOR. The minimum is a signed, written statement from each company. A member of a joint venture would normally confirm that it is prepared to associate with the other member companies for the purposes of the specified project, and name the lead company. Sub-consultants would confirm that they are prepared to associate with the lead company (or other member of the joint venture) for the purposes of the specified project. Freelance arrangements are not usually included in this section unless the freelancer concerned has such a good reputation with the client that it is worth emphasising his involvement with the team.

In a TOR, association *arrangements* can have a wider meaning than association *agreements*. Some clients (and some TOR) may want more than a straightforward declaration of association. They may expect the consultants to explain what arrangements they have made to divide the work, or they may ask for details of how the international consultant intends to provide the technology transfer to the local partner company. Only the client can tell you what he means by the phrase.

The TOR may also include other, explicit requirements, such as asking consultants to include a signed copy of the TOR in their proposal documents.

Information not relevant to the client

Some details of the association arrangements need to be settled between the partner companies, but do not need to be passed on to the client.

Where the lead company is able to carry out the project work alone, using only its own staff, then it is easy to remember the details of the association arrangements (there aren't any). For larger, more complex projects the association arrangements can include any number of joint venture partners, sub-consultants and freelancers. In these cases it can be difficult to recall who is associating with whom, and it is worthwhile preparing an *association chart* (Fig. 12)

- While this sort of graphic is not necessary for the formal proposal documents, it does help everyone in the partner companies understand who is associating with whom. The financial proposal may have to provide different information about each level of association.
- *joint and several liability* is a feature of joint venture agreements, as for example

> In a joint venture all parties to the Agreement will have considerable influence on the working decisions of the team and will almost always carry joint and several liability. Many clients see this as a major advantage of a joint venture.[49]

The phrase apparently means that if one joint venture partner produces poor work, *any other partner* can be forced to pay the full financial costs of putting it right. Companies with only a small involvement in the project might prefer to work as a sub-consultant. They should certainly make sure they have appropriate insurance cover. Joint and several liability is a real problem, but it can be relieved by having mutual clauses giving a 'duty of care to each other'. This would mean that the paying partner had the automatic right to sue the defaulting partner. Generally, joint venture partners should be of equal standing.

Documented arrangements are helpful to your own company's interests as well as to provide evidence for the client. It is not unknown for partner companies to pull out from a joint venture proposal at the last minute, or to make a similar agreement with two

---

49 FIDIC *Guide to the use of FIDIC's sub-consultancy and Joint Venture (consortium) agreements*, page 3, 1994 edition.

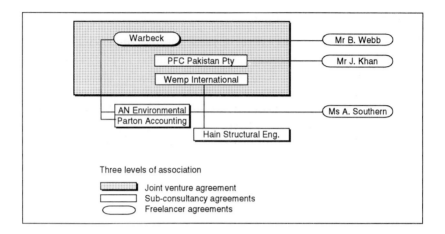

Company lists

Lead	Other·main	Sub-consultants	Freelancers
Warbeck UK	PFC Pakistan Pty	AN Environmental Studies	Ms A. Southern (environmentalist)
	Wemp International	Parton Accounting	Mr J. Khan (materials engineer)
		Hain Structural Eng. Ltd	Mr B. Webb (geologist)

(All these names are invented for the purposes of this figure)

While this sort of graphic is not necessary for the formal proposal documents, it does help everyone in the partner companies understand who is associating with whom. The financial proposal may have to provide different information about each level of association.

Fig. 12. Association arrangements

competitors for the same project. FIDIC has a sample form of pre-contract agreement to cover points like these.[50]

Preparing proposals for international projects can be very expensive, and the lead company may want to share the financial risks with its partners and sub-consultants. In such cases it is always more pleasant to specify the cost-sharing arrangements before submitting the proposal, rather than afterwards (and is another reason for keeping track of the costs). Normal practice is currently for each company to bear its own costs during pre-agreement work such as proposal preparation.

---

50   Annex to FIDICs *Guide to the use of FIDIC's sub-consultancy and joint venture (consortium) agreements,* 1994 edition.

Summary

- Provide the client with the information he asks for (answer the question).
- Keep track of your association arrangements.
- Keep track of your and your partner companies' costs.
- Arrange some form of written undertaking with your partner companies, covering points such as exclusivity, confidentiality, and cost-sharing — it is in your interests as much as it is in the client's.
- Keep your partner companies informed of progress.

Section 15.   Estimates of local facilities

Description

Purpose of this section

- To list the local facilities which the project team will need.
- To provide the remaining base information for the financial proposal.

Priority

★★★ This section has to wait until you have finished the notes on approach and methodology and the work programme.

Resources

People: team leader, businessman, country expert
Time: negligible to 2 weeks, depending on what information the site visit produced

Links to other Sections

11. Work programme

Discussion

The extent of local facilities which the project will require depends on the size and scope of the project. One expert travelling in-country for three months will need somewhat less material than a project calling for a 20-strong team of experts on a four-year assignment. You and your colleagues on the proposals team will have to make your own detailed assessment for each proposal. Your assessment should be reasonably accurate: if your assessment is *too high* the proposal becomes less competitive; *too low*, and you will be paying for the extra facilities out of the profits. It can help to divide the facilities into a few different types, and use these as the common starter for each proposal.

Local staff

These fall into three groups (Table 32). The first are the local professional staff. Some or all of these may be among the key

Table 32. *Examples of local facilities (a) local support staff*

Local professional staff	Technical support staff	Non-technical support staff
Engineers	Laboratory technicians	Secretary/typists
Economists	Survey assistants	Receptionists
Environmentalists	Traffic interviewers	Drivers
Sociologists	Draughtsmen	Guards
	Translators/interpreters	Tea-boys, messengers

personnel you propose for the project, and so you would need to name them and include their CV in the document. The second group are the technical support staff, such as materials laboratory technicians, draughtsmen and field survey assistants. The third group, the non-technical support staff, includes typists, receptionists, guards and messengers. You need the advice of the country expert and local partner to decide how many people in this third group (if any), your project will need.

Local equipment

This can also be sorted into groups, under the headings of transport, accommodation, and equipment (Table 33). The technical experts should be able to advise on the equipment which the project team will need. These days an important part is often computer-related equipment (hardware — including printers and plotters; software licences etc). You will need to have some idea of what the client and the local partner use either to make your site equipment compatible with theirs, or to suggest what new equipment they will need to make their system compatible with yours. Technology transfer is a frequent key theme of international proposals, and it doesn't work too well if the local computers cannot run your programs.

Table 33. *Examples of local facilities (b) local equipment*

Transport	Accommodation	Equipment and operating costs*
Cars	Head offices	Computer hardware
Pick-ups/4WD	Site offices	Computer software
Motorcycles	Residential living	Laboratory equipment
Other	• short-term international	Survey equipment
	• long-term int. (single)	Office furnishings
	• long-term int. (family)	Residential furnishings
	• local staff out-of-office	Telephone charges
		Sub-contracts*
		etc.

* *Plus* whatever the TOR specifically asks the consultants to describe and estimate.
* For example, sub-contracted site investigations.

Accommodation can also be a major factor. Poor facilities can mean that the site team does not have room to work in, and that the long-term expert walks out on the project as soon as he sees what you have chosen for his family accommodation. For this reason, you usually cannot leave the selection and, therefore, *costing* of local accommodation to your local partner. His idea of acceptable accommodation may be very different from yours and your colleagues on the project team. You will also need to consider which personnel will be on short- or long-term assignment, married or single status, as this will affect the type and costs of accommodation the project team will require.

Summary

- You need these estimates for the financial proposal, whether the TOR asks for them or not.
- You cannot rely on a local company to assess what will or will not be suitable accommodation and equipment.

Section 16. Appendices/other material

Description

Purpose of this section

- To serve as a store for material which supports some of the notes in the main body of the document.

Priority

★ This is one of the last sections which you prepare.

Resources

People: team leader
Time: negligible

Links to other sections

1–16. (all)

Discussion

There may be occasions when you want to back up some of your arguments in the main body of the document. Perhaps someone in your company has published a paper on technology transfer, for example. It would be out of place to put it in the section on key themes, but would be useful confirmation of your company's competence in the subject. You could add a copy of the article as an appendix. In some cases, it may also be worthwhile to add company brochures in the appendix — but these will be rare. After all, the client already knows enough about your company to have selected it for his proposals short list; and in some cases the TOR will specifically instruct you *not* to include brochures in your proposals documents.

Summary

- Use the appendices carefully — don't have too many, and don't include irrelevant material such as brochures.

Summary

The TOR which you have to follow may specify a different document structure and headings to those suggested in the preceding notes, but you will almost certainly still have to provide the same sort of detail. Table 34 lists again the main parts of the technical proposal, and summarises

- what priority you should give them
- which ones provide the input to the financial proposal
- which ones you should already have available as modules.

Table 35 suggests where you and the proposals team should put most of your effort — and where you shouldn't.

Summary — writing technical proposals

- Save time and trouble by using pre-prepared modules.
- Concentrate your effort on the sections which can win you the most points.

Table 34. Technical proposal — summary of chapter priorities

Document part or chapter	Priority	Links to financial proposal	Suitable as modules
1. Title page, edge page	★	⇐	✔
2. Submission letter	★	⇐	
3. Table of contents	★★★		✔
4. Introduction	★		
5. Company description	★★		✔
6. Site appreciation	★★★★		
7. Project appreciation	★★★★		
8. Approach and methodology (1)—task lists	★★★★		
9. Approach and methodology (2)—technical notes	★★★		
10. Approach and methodology (3)—key themes	★★★	⇐	✔
11. Work programme	★★★★	⇐	✔
12. Comments on the TOR	★★		
13. Staff CVs	★★★★	⇐	✔
14. Association agreements	★★★★	⇐	✔
15. Estimates of local facilities	★★★	⇐	
16. Appendices/other material	★		

Note. Parts 5 to 13 are the core of the technical proposal.

Table 35.   Technical proposal — amount of effort to be spent on each chapter

Element	Wrong %	Right %
Beginning (sections 1–4)	10	–
The core of the technical proposal		
5. Company description	30	10
6–10. Appreciation and Methodology Approach	30	20
11. Work programme	10	30
12. Comments on the TOR	–	–
13. Staff CVs	10	30
Loose ends (sections 14–16)	10	10
Total	100	100

Notes. Most of the evaluation points go to the sections on CVs, the work programme and the approach and methodology, in that order. You should put most of your effort into these sections.

- Use a clear and consistent text style and document layout — if the reviewer can't find the information he is looking for he won't award it any points.
- Only five sections have top priority: the site and project appreciations, the task lists, work programme and the staff CVs; don't leave these until the last minute, *do* complete them first.

7

Writing financial proposals

Introduction

If you have now almost finished the first draft of the technical proposal, you should have enough basic information to begin work on the most important part of the proposal documents: the financial proposal. This point is worth repeating. The financial proposal is *more important* than the technical proposal. A good technical proposal can win your company the project, but a bad financial proposal can mean your company wins the project but loses a fortune, and maybe even goes bankrupt in the process. You and your company do not want to take on new work if it means losing money. The only exception is where you plan to lose money, because you see the project as a loss-leader, as a means to get your company established in the target country. Even here, the careful consultant has a good idea of how much money he plans to lose, before he begins to risk it.

There is an argument that the financial proposal only needs to give a rough idea of the eventual costs of the project. The reasoning is that the selected consultant can always argue out the details during the contract negotiations. If rough means 'to within 95% accuracy', then the argument is acceptable. Otherwise it is nonsense, for a number of reasons

(a)   over estimates can lose you the project
(b)   under estimates can lose your company money
(c)   inaccurate estimates can make your company look incompetent.

Overestimates can lose you the project   Many clients rank proposals based on a combination of their evaluations of the technical and financial proposals — even when they should not. For example, many IFIs require that the consultant submit the technical and financial proposals in separate, sealed documents.

- *The two-envelope system:* in this form of the system, the technical proposals are evaluated first, and the leading consultant invited to negotiate a contract. In theory, the client only opens his financial proposal at the start of the negotiations. In practice, many clients will open the financial proposals first, and have nothing more to do with the most expensive ones.
- *The cost-weighted system:*[51] in this system, a comparison of the costs of the different financial proposals follows the technical evaluation; the results are combined (for example, in a ratio of 85% technical score: 15% financial cost). If your financial proposal is unnecessarily high, it will take points away from the technical proposal.

Under-estimates can lose your company money Contract negotiations certainly do give the selected consultant some room to manoeuvre (which is why they are called negotiations). However, the businessman can only negotiate on the basis of an accurate financial proposal. For example, the financial proposal may underestimate the cost of local accommodation (perhaps the proposals team forgot to allow for electricity and water charges). Since this underestimate was a mistake, the businessman is not aware of it and will not argue for corrected figures during the negotiations. Your company will have to pay for the forgotten costs out of its own profit.

Inaccurate estimates can make your company look incompetent It is not always possible to argue away minor errors in the financial proposal during contract negotiations. Some TOR state that the financial proposal *as submitted* will form a formal part of the contract. Even where the TOR are less definitive, the client is not going to look warmly on a consultant who says that his cost estimates are (say) 30% in error. The corrected figure may upset the consultant's ranking. It will certainly make the consultant look incompetent. The client will ask if the consultant is likely to make as bad a job of carrying out the project as he did of the financial proposal.

---

51 For notes on both systems, see FIDIC's *Guidelines on quality-based selection of consulting engineers*, page 7, 1991.

Basic techniques

Understanding the problem

At first sight the financial proposal may seem much more difficult to prepare than the technical proposal. It covers so many, non-engineering terms such as social charges, overhead costs, per diem, and so on. In fact financial proposals can be quite easy, once you understand the problem. One way of doing this is to sort the main elements of the financial proposal into some sort of structure. Some TOR encourage this, as they ask consultants to provide separate estimates of

(*a*)   foreign currency, local currency and base currency costs
(*b*)   remuneration, out-of-pocket expenses and contingencies
(*c*)   for remuneration, details of basic salary, social charges and overhead costs, and profit.

Foreign, local currency and base currency costs   The project will involve you spending money in at least two different currencies: your own, and that of the target country. Most financial proposals will involve more than this — perhaps you have set up a joint venture where one member comes from a third country. While it would be helpful if the different types of expense, could be sorted, by definition, into those which will only involve the international currency, and those which will only involve the local currency, it is not possible in practice. For example, the proposed key personnel may include international staff and engineers from a local partner company; air travel costs may include travel for your company's key staff from your country to the project country (international currency), or business trips within the country (local currency), or international business trips where the project involves cross-border studies (international or local currency).

   Financial proposals for international projects will involve a mix of currencies. The consultants that the client has invited to submit a proposal will probably come from a number of countries, giving rise to another mix of currencies. Some TOR will therefore ask consultants to convert their cost estimates into a common, base currency such as US dollars. This will help the client compare the various financial proposals.

   • *Local currency:* the currency of the country in which the project is to be carried out. Where the project is to be carried out in more than one country, there can be more than one local currency.

- *Foreign currency*: the currency of the consultant's home country. Where the consultant is a JV group whose members come from more than one country, there can be more than one foreign currency.
- *Base currency*: currency quoted in the financial proposal which is used to provide common units and totals of the foreign and local cost estimates.

Remuneration, out-of-pocket expenses and contingencies

- *Remuneration*: all that consultants have to offer is expertise. They do not make computers, or bridges (contractors build bridges, consultants design them), or any other physical object. The expertise is supplied by the individual experts on the consultant's staff; remuneration is the payment which the client makes for the direct use of these individuals. Remuneration is often split into

  - basic salaries
  - social charges
  - overhead costs
  - fees (profit).

- *Out-of-pocket expenses*: these are the indirect costs of hiring the individual members of the consultant's staff. For example, you might be delighted if someone offered to pay you to work in Hong Kong for six months, but your delight would be rather less if you had to pay for your air ticket and accommodation yourself. Clients repay these costs without any percentage mark-up as a fee or profit. Out-of-pocket expenses can be sub-divided into

  - per diem
  - transport
  - accommodation
  - equipment (owning costs, operating costs)
  - insurance, tax
  - administration costs.

- *Contingencies*: a lump sum or percentage of total detailed costs which provides for unexpected and unforeseen expenses. Some TOR make specific provision for this, and allow it to be spent only on further written approval by the client. Even where the TOR do not mention contingencies, you should consider making some sort of provision for them; you are unlikely to prepare a perfectly accurate financial estimate.

Basic salary, social charges and overhead costs   All clients want to know how much the consultant will charge them for the services of their key personnel. Some clients, perhaps in an excess of accounting zeal, not only ask for these costs (for the monthly remuneration per individual) but also require an explanation of how it is made up. Remuneration includes the company's profit or fee; it can also be split into basic salaries, social charges and overhead costs. Briefly,

- *basic salaries* are what appears in the individual staff members' pay packets
- *social charges* are other staff-related payments, such as company contributions towards pension schemes and annual leave costs
- *overhead costs* are non-staff specific operating costs; for example, a consultant may employ 20 urban studies engineers — to do this he needs to rent and furnish offices for them, and provide administrative support staff such as secretaries and accountants.

Detailed lists and structures Figure 13 gives an overview of the various main headings under (a) to (c) above. In practice, they can each be broken down still further, as Table 36 shows. Unfortunately, it is not yet possible to give one, universally-applicable, list of the elements which can make up the final financial proposal. The reason is that different clients and consultants give different definitions of the various elements. Where they do agree on a meaning for an element, clients can place different rules on it. As an example, an overseas allowance could be either

- an extra, incentive payment to individual staff, which is meant to encourage them to accept the chance of working outside their own home country, and away from family and friends or

Table 36. Elements of the financial proposal (examples)

Level 1	Level 2	Level 3	Level 4	Level 5
Out-of-pocket expenses	Transport	International (air)	Air travel for international staff	Air tickets for contract start and leave trips
Out-of-pocket expenses	Type of accommodation	Residential	Residential accommodation for international staff	For international staff on long-term, single status contracts
Out-of-pocket expenses	Insurance	Staff	Medical insurance	Local or international; single or family

Note. For more detailed lists see check lists 6 to 8.

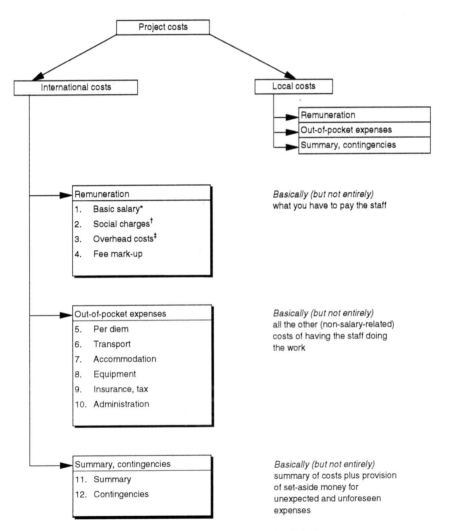

Fig. 13.   Main elements of the financial proposal

- an allowance to cover the additional personal costs of living and working in a foreign country (local personal transport costs, personal international telephone calls, local food costs etc.).

The TOR may state that the client is unwilling to pay for staff incentives, but is prepared to contribute to a cost of living allowance. The consultant then either provides an inflated figure for the latter, or hides the cost of the incentive partly in the cost of living allowance, and partly in the company overheads and other elements of his financial proposal. Alternatively, the incentives become a charge on the firm's profit and loss account (rather than an operating cost).

Check lists 6 to 8 attempt to give some idea of all the various elements which make up the financial proposal.

Software/spreadsheets

The key people working on the financial proposal will be the team leader, the businessman and the accountant. At least one of them (and preferably the team leader) should be familiar with the use of spreadsheets. While the task of developing and updating the spreadsheets could be done by a technician, the meagre benefits of saving an engineer's time are often far outweighed by disbenefits such as

- more chance of errors (through misunderstanding or poor communication)
- lost time (telling someone else how to do something can take longer than doing it yourself)
- poorer understanding of the financial effects of any decisions the proposals team may have made (less finger-tip control).

The value of spreadsheets is that, set up properly, they can calculate the effect of any changes in cost or resource estimates within a few seconds, through the whole financial proposal. These changes may be either technical or business. *Technical* changes are where the proposals team change the staffing programme, or where someone hears of recent increases in air travel costs. *Business* changes are where the businessman decides to reduce the quoted fee rate, or to quote a loss-making rate on the local staff costs. Conventional spreadsheets also allow the information they contain to be presented in the same style and quality as the text pages of the technical and financial proposals.

One way of developing the spreadsheets is to show each of the main elements of the financial proposal in separate tables (Fig. 14). The tables should follow a clear structure (preferably one which you have developed from your understanding of the problem) and ideally cover no more than one page each. Some TOR insist that consultants use the table layout which they (the TOR) propose. This doesn't mean that the TOR tables are particularly clear, but simply that the reviewer is used to them and will see the same layout in all the submitted proposals. Whatever structure you use in the tables, you should use the same structure in the text notes of your financial proposal.

Twin documents

There are a number of main purposes behind most financial proposals. First of all you want to estimate the total cost of the services you propose to offer, and to show the client how you arrive at this figure. Later on, the client may want to extend the project, and a detailed financial proposal can provide the rates for the extra work. The financial proposal will also help the proposals team leader as he develops his initial work programme; and later on, it will remind you and your colleagues how you actually estimated the cost of the services.

This can be particularly important where the actual costs of the services may be different to the ones you quote to the client. There are various reasons for this. The most obvious one is where the

Traffic Studies Project, Ruritania					Financial Proposal

Table 1: Transport

Item	Number	Unit cost, currency			Base
		Foreign (1)	Foreign (2)	Local	
Foreign currency costs					
1.1 2nd class return tickets, UK – Ruritania	2	1000·0	—	—	
1.2 2nd class return tickets, D – Ruritania	1	—	2500·0	—	
	Total	2000·0	2500·0	—	3000·0
Local currency costs					
2.1 Transport from airport to site office	4	—	—	40·5	
	Total	—	—	162·0	658·0

Notes

1   The particular layout shown is not particularly important. What *is* important is the need to follow a clear structure, both *within* the tables and *between* the tables.

2   The item numbers provide a coat-hook to hang explanatory notes on. These notes should normally be added to the text part of the document, rather than as footnotes to the tables themselves.

Fig. 14. Sample financial table

consulting company wants to establish itself in the target country. One way of increasing its chance of winning the project is to offer a low price — to make a loss on this particular project with the hope of winning many more, more profitable ones, later on. The company then uses the project as a loss-leader. Sometimes the TOR are unreasonable. For example, the client may refuse to pay more than the salary which the key personnel receive for working in their own country — forgetting that these people expect some additional compensation for spending months away from their family or friends, often working for very long hours in less than comfortable surroundings. Or perhaps the client will not pay for the leave costs where the leave is taken during the period of the service (rather than at the end of it). Finally, and perhaps, more rarely, the consultant may wish to recover the costs of paying incentives to local middlemen.

In a way, accounting is rather like statistics, in that you choose to present the accounts/statistics which best suit the point you are trying to make. For sound, honourable business reasons you may need to present the accounts to the client in one way, and to yourself and your colleagues in another. It is possible to do this in the same spreadsheet tables, but safer to do so either in separate spreadsheets, or in a twin financial proposal document.

Sources of information

There are two types of information which you need: information on resources and costs. *Resources* include the staff who will be working on the project, the number and duration of their assignments; the return air tickets they will need; their accommodation, and so on. The *costs* are the unit rates for each of these resources. The sources of this information include

- *the technical proposal*. The staffing schedule, staff lists and estimates of local facilities are the primary source of resource information. Whatever other information it shows, the financial proposal must be consistent with the figures in the technical proposal.
- *direct interviews*. If you forgot to check directly with the key personnel, now is the time to ask them whether they have any special requirements for this project. The information can change your resource and cost estimates. For example, they might want to travel with their family, and so expect married status accommodation, and perhaps extra payments for the local costs of their children's education; or they may ask for more money, where the target country is not a particularly safe or pleasant country to

work in. You may have to reflect some of these changes in the appropriate parts of the technical proposal.

- *the site visit.* Provided the right questions were asked, the site visit should give you a reliable idea of the cost of suitable office and residential accommodation for the international staff.
- *your company's local office.* Resident international staff are the most reliable sources of information on local costs.
- *the local partner.* He will be able to advise on the number, type and costs of local resources such as support staff, but will be less reliable when he has to identify and estimate the costs of suitable accommodation and furnishings for the international staff.
- *company accounts.* These are the main source of costs such as staff salaries, and overheads. Some TOR require consultants to provide certified copies of the company accounts as proof of the figures they quote in the financial proposal.
- *travel agents.* Your company's pet travel agent should be able to give the best advice on costs such as air tickets and hotel accommodation.
- *other sources.* For example, the *Economist Intelligence Unit* publishes cost of living surveys for over 80 countries around the world. The information includes costs of renting local housing and apartments, notes on the availability of local schooling, and details such as car operating expenses, hotel costs, and the local inflation rate.
- *other proposals.* Why re-invent the wheel; if your company has recently prepared other proposals for the target country, they are likely to contain just the information you are looking for.

Financial proposals team

The same people who work on the technical proposal should also work on the financial proposal, but a different selection will be asked to take centre stage. These key people are

(a)　*team leader.* The team leader is responsible for seeing that the technical and financial proposals are ready on time and within the budget, and that they agree with each other.

(b)　*businessman.* He will have to collect details of local costs from his contacts in the target country, provide advice (e.g. on what is suitable and unsuitable accommodation), and chase confidential company information and desired fee levels from the other members of the JV group.

(c) *accountant.* The accountant has to provide most of the cost estimates, and provide an explanation of them for the client, and for the company management.

(d) *management support.* This person has to advise on what profit level the company is prepared to accept for this particular project, whether it should be a loss-leader, and on the share of profit or loss with other members of the JV group.

Time to prepare the financial proposal

The financial proposal will take you as long to prepare as the technical proposal, since changes in one will normally lead to changes in the other. In terms of *working* time rather than *calendar* time, provided you have

- pre-prepared spreadsheets
- a complete draft technical proposal
- full information on local and international costs

then you should be able to prepare the draft financial proposal within two to four days.

Document administration

The same rules apply for the financial as for the technical proposals.

- You should keep a master copy of the financial proposal.
- The page layout and text style should be the same as for the technical proposal.

Financial proposal structure and contents

The financial proposal has four main sections. The first, small section includes the title page and the cover letter. The next section includes all the text notes which give background details to some of the costs, proposal methods and instalments of payments, discusses ways of allowing for possible price or cost inflation, and so on. The third section includes all the detailed financial tables, normally presented in the manner and order which the TOR specify. The final section includes all the supporting documentation which the TOR demand and require at this stage (they may note that the consultant will have to provide even more supporting material during the contract negotiations). The following summary gives an overview of the structure of a financial proposal

- introduction
    - ◦ title page, edge page
    - ◦ background notes
    - ◦ copy of staffing schedule
- the tables
    - ◦ remuneration
        1. basic salaries
        2. social charges
        3. overhead costs
        4. fee mark-up
    - ◦ out-of-pocket expenses
        5. per diem
        6. transport
        7. accommodation
        8. equipment
        9. insurance
        10. administration
    - ◦ summary, contingencies
        11. summary
        12. contingencies
- appendices/other material
    - ◦ certified company accounts.

The main sections of the financial proposal

The following sections discuss in turn each of the main sections of the financial proposal shown in Table 37.

Description

The notes list the various items of expenditure which you should consider in this particular section.

Discussion

Notes on some of the items of expenditure listed under description.

Things which may go wrong

It can sometimes be difficult to see financial information in terms of engineering reality. These notes give examples of problems which may occur if you do not pay enough attention to the financial proposal.

Table 37.   *Structure and content of the financial proposal*

Main section	Typical contents	
Introduction		
Introduction	Title page, edge page	Table of contents
	Submission letter	
Background	Payment schedule	Inflation clauses
notes	Arbitration and mediation	Legal language
	Copy of staffing schedule	Legal jurisdiction
Remuneration		
1. Basic	Key personnel	Local key personnel
salaries	Backstoppers	Local technical support
(rates at		staff
man–		Local non-technical
months)		support staff
2. Social	Leave	Social expenses
charges	Financial benefits	Miscellaneous
3. Overhead	Buildings and equipment	Professional expenses
costs	Consumables	Miscellaneous
	Non-billable staff	
4. Fee mark-up	Fee mark-up, profit	
Out-of-pocket		
5. Per diem.	Overseas allowance	Education costs
	Bonus	Local staff travel per diem
	Travel per diem	Local staff residential
	Residential per diem	per diem
6. Transport	International transport (air)	Local transport (air)
	International transport	Local transport (road)
	(road)	
7. Accommo-	Travel accommodation	Office accommodation
dation	Residential accommodation	
8. Equipment	Accommodation furnishings	Computer hardware,
	Office furnishings	software
9. Insurance,	Staff medical insurance	Company tax
tax	Company insurance	Income tax
	Emergency insurance	Special contributions*
10. Adminis-	Telephone	E-mail, Internet
tration	Document reproduction	Staff medical certificates
	Document postage	Visas and permits
Summary		
11. Summary	Foreign currency(s)	Local currency
tables	Base currency	
12. Contingen-		
cies		
Appendices		
	Certified company accounts	
	Key staff salary statements	

* Special contributions, such as Germany's reunification tax and some Middle Eastern countries' support for Palestine contributions.

Background notes

Typical contents

Notes on

- business and tax laws of the country of operation
- arbitration/mediation
- exchange rates
- price escalation

  - allow for exchange rates changes
  - allow for inflation
  - allow for changes in labour costs (direct and indirect, social charges, salaries etc.)

- method of payment
- currency of payment
- contingencies
- ruling language
- governing law
- local income tax, company tax
- backstopping services.

Discussion

The main purpose of the background notes is to cover contractual matters which may have been left unclear in the TOR, or which you do not entirely agree with. Whether the client agrees to accept your new explanation is a matter for the financial negotiations, but if you fail to mention them here you may find it difficult to bring them up later on. For example, the TOR may not mention any financial compensation to the consultant should exchange rates vary during the course of the project. You may not want to specify a detailed corrective formula now, but could still usefully make some sort of holding statement along the lines that

> the consultant will resolve questions of corrective formulae for exchange rates, during the contract negotiations.

Questions concerning local income tax and company tax, can often be a big problem.

Things which may go wrong

- The tax laws of the country are changed during the period of the contract.
- The client specifies two ruling languages for the project.
- The consultant forgets to ask for a start-up payment.
- Both the client and the consultant omit to specify any method of arbitration.
- The client decides to hold 20% of the fees as retention money during a two-year maintenance period at the end of the project.
- The TOR do not mention payment for backstopping services, and the consultant omits to allow for them (either directly, or within his figure for overhead costs).

Remuneration: 1. Basic salaries

Description

Details for

- types of staff
  - ° sub-consultants
  - ° freelance
- key personnel
  - ° foreign key personnel
  - ° local key personnel
  - ° backstoppers
- support staff
  - ° technical support
  - ° non-technical support.

Discussion

Types of staff

All the various details of remuneration — basic salaries, social charges, fee mark-ups and so on — can be shown in one table, where one row of the table relates to a particular member of the key personnel. The details will vary with each person, not only because each will probably be earning a different salary but also people working for different companies will have different social charges and fee mark-ups associated with them. The TOR may also require less detailed information, for example on staff from sub-consultants. The lead consultant may want to charge a different fee for any freelancers which he wishes to employ.

Key personnel

The key personnel will probably include both foreign and local staff. While the client may expect to pay the cost of some sort of overseas incentive for the former, he certainly will not for the latter. Where you or the TOR decide to detail the cost of backstopping services, you should also include details of these people here.

Support staff

The costs of the consultants normal support staff will be covered by his estimates of overhead charges. This item relates to the full-time, local support staff who will be employed solely for this project. You will have to give a detailed breakdown of the remuneration rates for support staff, but nevertheless you should remember to include an element of profit, as well as their full total costs to you or your local partner.

Things which may go wrong

- You forget to allow for staff incentives, and forget generally to ask your colleagues what additional salary they will expect if they have to work in the target country.
- When preparing a proposal for a long-term project, you omit to allow for annual staff salary increments.
- You quote a different figure to the one shown on the staff's salary slips, in cases where the TOR request copies of these as supporting material.

Remuneration: 2. Social charges

Description

Details for

- leave
  - ○ statutory holidays
  - ○ emergency leave
  - ○ sick leave
  - ○ vacation leave
  - ○ local public holidays
  - ○ religious holidays

- financial benefits
  - ○ bonus/incentive
  - ○ company/car loan
  - ○ 13th month pay (for experts from some countries)
  - ○ meal allowances

- social expenses
  - ○ social security contributions
  - ○ retirement/ superannuation
  - ○ health and medical expenses

- miscellaneous
  - ○ education/training benefits.

Discussion

Leave

As with most parts of the financial proposal, what you decide to include in this section will depend on the requirements of the TOR and the advice of your accountant and business colleagues. For example, by removing leave from social charges you could justify invoicing for twelve months per year where staff are on long-term assignment, or you could simply bill for time on site. Further, the notes on social charges are meant to represent the normal, home-based costs of the staff concerned and so should not normally include elements such as emergency leave. Nevertheless, you as proposals team leader should make sure that you have considered their costs somewhere in the financial proposal.

- Statutory holidays are paid public holidays, which vary from country to country.

- vacation leave is the normal annual holiday which the individual is typically entitled to.
- Sick leave is the typical number of days staff take off each year on the grounds of illness. In detail some TOR will specify the maximum number of days sick leave which an expert is entitled to before the client either refuses to pay for him, or demands a replacement. You should make sure that such the possibility of someone becoming seriously ill or dying, while working on the project, is covered by the company or project insurance.
- Emergency leave is *not* an item covered by the heading social charges, but one covered by the term leave — you should ensure the eventuality is covered by appropriate insurance.
- Local public holidays are as for emergency leave; the client may not object to project staff taking local public holidays, both you and the client would object if the project staff insist on taking both their home country public holidays and the local ones.
- Religious holidays. Home country religious holidays are covered by the statutory holidays. For local public holidays, project staff will in practice be entitled to take one and not the other.

Financial benefits

A heading covering miscellaneous social charges, which are often those invented by the company and its staff as a means of tax-avoiding replacements for direct increases in salary.

Social expenses

Other elements of direct, staff-related costs.

Things which may go wrong

- A close relative of one of the key experts dies while the expert is working in the target country, and you have not made any financial allowance for his emergency leave, emergency travel costs and temporary replacement.

Remuneration: 3. Overhead costs

Description

Details for

- buildings and equipment (*home office only!*)
  - rent
  - amortisation expense
  - repairs and maintenance
  - depreciation expense
  - utilities
  - office furnishings and equipment

- consumables
  - data processing
  - communication and postage
  - office supplies, printing

- non-billable staff
  - administration staff
  - international representatives
  - partners

- professional costs
  - professional fees
  - professional training
  - research and development

- miscellaneous
  - advertising, promotions
  - taxes, licences, permits
  - travel and transportation
  - insurances.

Discussion

Costs which are associated with running a professional consulting office. As with the social charges, the figures are meant to explain and justify the total remuneration which your company shows for each of its key personnel. The client may wish to see the figures in order to satisfy himself that the fee or profit you are charging him for each of the key personnel is not excessive, although some might suggest that this is not relevant to his decision. Once you have prepared detailed lists of both social charges and overhead costs, you should have sets of accounts which you can use for other, future proposals. In each case, however, you may wish to review the figures in terms of other specific requests of the client for financial information.

Many clients will accept an average rate for social charges and overhead costs, each average based on the company's average total annual professional fee compared with its total annual social charge or overhead cost.

Non-billable staff

These are the normal secretarial and other office staff who provide the normal, year-round support services for your company, and hence for its staff of professional consultants. You can normally identify and invoice separately for project-specific support staff; these will almost always be staff employed in the target country. Rare exceptions might be technical document translators.

Miscellaneous

Your accountant should make sure that the accounts cover somewhere the costs of company taxes and insurances.

Things which may go wrong

- Your accountant prepares different details of overhead costs, which are presented in two separate proposals, but both for the same client.

Remuneration: 4. Fee mark-up

Description

Details for

- fees and profit.

Discussion

Fees and profit — which are basically the same — is the money which your company will make by providing the consulting services for the new project. Clients will not normally accept a consultant making any profit on out-of-pocket expenses, such as the purchase of air tickets for the key personnel. Some may also object to consultants charging profit for providing local support staff, although this seems less defensible.

Your company's net earnings depend, therefore, on the percentage it makes on the staff remuneration (the fee mark-up) and here the businessman, the accountant and the proposals advisor need to consider.

- how much fee to charge which would still make the total project cost interesting both to the client and to your company.
- whether creative accountancy could draw more returns for your company from the same total project cost.

Things which may go wrong

- You quote a percentage fee mark-up which is outside the limits acceptable to the client and specified in the TOR (an acceptable figure would be around 10–15%).

Out-of-pocket expenses: 5. Per diem

Description

Details for

- travel per diem
    - international staff
    - local staff
- residential per diem
    - international staff
    - local staff
- other
    - bonus
    - housing allowance
    - overseas allowance
    - education allowance.

Discussion

Travelling to and working in another country would involve you in a variety of minor costs, besides the comparatively major expenses of accommodation and travel. Examples might be purchase of meals and light refreshments, laundry and dry cleaning costs, and local private transport (bus, tram). You would expect your company to reimburse these expenses, and your company in turn would reclaim their costs from the client without, of course, any added element of profit. This type of personal out-of-pocket costs are called per diem, and are a daily personal allowance.

What would seem reasonable to your key staff will probably also seem reasonable to local key personnel and support staff. In preparing the financial proposal, you should check whether some sort of daily personal allowance or reimbursement will also have to be made for the local staff.

Some banks issue standard tables which give their accepted per diem rates for different target countries (some governments in Western Europe do the same). Where the TOR for your project do not include specific per diem rates, you may want to use other standard tables as a guide, such as the UN per diem book.

There is a second reason for per diem payments, and one which is quite unconnected with minor costs and expenses: per diem payments can be used as a form of cash incentive to key staff, particularly where the TOR frowns on other forms such as increased salary, bonus, and overseas allowance. What you decide to pay individual staff (and how you choose to describe it) depends on the TOR, your accountant, and the staff concerned.

Travel per diem

This can include

- allowance for key personnel's start-up travel from their home country to the target country
- during the project, allowance for travel from the site office on business meetings
- allowance for key personnel's leave travel
- allowance for members of the key personnel's family, if he is on a married-status assignment.

Residential per diem

This is a daily allowance for staff who are working away from their home base for a short period of time (short being defined as anything from a few days to six months, depending on the TOR).

Other

Some TOR may specify a different rate of daily allowance for staff who will be working away from their home base for longer periods of time. Individual staff may also have their own expectations, which may not entirely agree with the provisions of the TOR. Whatever their name, they are a form of cash incentive or compensation which should first be agreed with the staff concerned, and then covered in detail somewhere in the financial proposal.

Things which may go wrong

- You forget to check with the key personnel what financial expectations they expect if they are to work in the target country.

Out-of-pocket expenses: 6. Transport

Description

Details for

- international (air)
    - start-up travel
    - leave travel
    - international staff
    - local staff
    - business travel
    - international staff (families)
    - airport taxes

- international (road)
    - international staff
    - international staff (families)

- local transport (air)
    - international staff
    - local staff
    - international staff (families)
    - airport taxes

- local transport (road)
    - vehicle type, numbers
    - fuel and oil
    - vehicle insurance, taxes
    - purchase or hire
    - maintenance and servicing

- personal luggage
    - accompanied
    - shipment of personal effects
    - unaccompanied

- equipment
    - air freight
    - surface freight.

Discussion

You should check that you include in the financial proposal *all* the transport costs which the project will involve, although you or the TOR may decide to put some elements under different headings.

International (Air)

Start-up and leave travel for international staff and their families, and for local staff; and airport taxes, overnight accommodation and the cost of travel from home or site to the international airport. Most TOR will accept only economy-class air travel.

International (Road)

Your staff may be able to reach some international destinations by road or rail, e.g. for EU-financed projects in Western and Central Europe.

Local transport (Air)

Alternatively, some projects may require staff to make journeys within the target country by air; many projects in the Peoples Republic of China will include this type of trip.

Local transport (Road)

Most international projects will involve the use of local road transport, both for key personnel and for local support staff. You should check that you quote for the appropriate number and type of vehicle, and include for the ancillary costs of vehicle insurance, taxes, fuel etc. In particular

- if purchasing outright, check whether the client expects you to hand the vehicles over to him at the end of the contract period
- check whether there is any restriction in the TOR on the use of site vehicles for personal use.

Personal luggage

The usual allowance of 20 kg of accompanied luggage will not be enough for anyone travelling on more than a two-week assignment; for longer periods some of the key personnel may expect a married status assignment, and you may have to include additional accompanied/unaccompanied luggage allowance for each member of their family, as well as providing some form of shipment for their personal effects.

Equipment

Your financial estimates should cover the cost of shipment of any equipment needed for the project, and any related customs, taxes and insurance charges; the costs will be different depending on whether the equipment is to be temporarily or permanently imported into the project country.

Things which may go wrong

- You don't leave enough time to consider all the transport costs which the project will incur.

Out-of-pocket expenses: 7. Accommodation

Description
Details for

- travel accommodation
    - ○ international hotel
    - ○ local hotel
- residential accommodation
    - ○ short-term foreign staff
    - ○ long-term foreign staff (single status)
    - ○ long-term foreign staff (married status)
    - ○ local staff (out of office)
- office accommodation
    - ○ local head office
    - ○ local site office
- general
    - ○ cost of services and taxes
    - ○ cost of cleaning and maintenance.

Discussion

You should check that you include in the financial proposal *all* the accommodation costs which the project will involve (or where you omit them, make sure that you do so deliberately, rather than by mistake).

Travel accommodation

Overnight accommodation during start-up and leave journeys for key professional staff and their families; hotel accommodation for local business trips; perhaps also temporary accommodation for visiting backstoppers.

Residential accommodation

This will depend on the mix and duration of assignments of the project staff. Staff on family-status assignments will expect an apartment of their own, probably furnished, and possibly including the cost of all services (gas, air-conditioning etc.). Those with young children may ask for a villa with garden, although whether this is a practicable idea will depend on the project location. Staff on single status may be prepared to stay in a hotel for a few weeks, following which they (or you) may prefer to provide either shared apartments, or a guest house (a guest house is a single building with one room for each person, plus communal recreation and eating areas, and usually with full-time cooking and cleaning staff).

You should generally have an idea of the approximate costs of the different types of suitable residential accommodation, before you begin the detailed work on the financial proposal.

Office accommodation

This should be adequate for all the project team — key personnel and support staff — *plus* space for

- meeting rooms
- reception rooms
- kitchen
- storage
- printing/copying.

As a rough guide, each person would need perhaps 6 to 10 sq.m. of office space (for more detailed estimates, a publication such as the *New metric handbook*[52] would be helpful).

General

You should remember to include the cost of electricity and other services, cleaning and maintenance, property taxes, security services etc.

Things which may go wrong

- The client agrees to provide you with adequate office accommodation; but his understanding of adequate is different from your own.
- Similarly, your local partner promises to provide you with adequate office accommodation, but his understanding of adequate is also different to yours.

---

52 *New metric handbook: planning and design data,* ed. Tutt and Adler, published by Butterworth Architecture.

Out-of-pocket expenses: 8. Equipment

Description

Details for

- furnishings
  - ○ residential
  - ○ office
- computers
  - ○ hardware
  - ○ software
- technical
  - ○ laboratory equipment
  - ○ survey equipment
- general
  - ○ local hire/local purchase
  - ○ permanent transfer
  - ○ customs and administration.

Discussion

Each project will include the consultant providing some equipment, either as office or residential furnishings, or technical equipment which will be needed by the surveying staff, laboratory staff, and so on. Where equipment could be a substantial part of the financial costs, you will want to check whether it is available locally for hire/purchase. Some TOR will require you to handover any purchased equipment at the end of the project, and this may affect your decision on what to provide and how to provide it.

Things which may go wrong

- You offer to give the client some of the equipment at the end of the project, while the TOR require you to leave it all.
- You include the cost of purchasing a photocopier, but forget to include the cost of the maintenance agreement and of the consumables for it (paper, ink).

Out-of-pocket expenses: 9. Insurance and taxes

Description

Details for

- insurance
    - staff medical insurance
    - local company insurance
    - professional liability insurance
    - equipment insurance
    - property insurance
    - staff emergency insurance
    - third party liability insurance
    - employer's liability insurance
    - business insurance

- Taxes
    - company tax
    - income tax
    - local taxes, duties, fees
    - special contributions.

Discussion

Insurance

The question of insurance is almost worth a book of its own; at the moment the best advice is to check it over with your company's general insurer and, for the local requirements, check either with your local office, the local partner, or with someone else who has experience of working in the target country.

For additional staff cover you should realise that people become ill, have accidents, and die all the time; they are at least as likely to do this while working on the project as when they are working from their home office. In some countries, risk of war or rebellion are additional hazards where staff may demand additional protection (such as your company laying on a special flight to take them out of the country) — hence the reference to staff emergency insurance.

Taxes

Many TOR for international projects state that the services will be exempted from local personal or company taxes. You should not take this for granted however — read the TOR and if they are not clear, ask the client to comment.

Things which may go wrong

- Project staff are kidnapped.
- Someone on the staff is injured in a traffic accident (a more likely event abroad than in the UK).
- The project office is damaged in a hurricane, and the data files damaged by water.

Out-of-pocket expenses: 10. Administration

Description

Details for

- telecommunications
    - telephone rental, usage
    - Email, Internet rental, usage
    - portable telephone rental, usage
    - other telecommunications

- documents
    - document reproduction
    - document postage

- staff administration
    - entry visas
    - work permits
    - local driving licence
    - residence visas
    - local medical checks, certificates
    - additional medical vaccinations

- translations
    - translation costs
    - interpreting costs.

Discussion

Telecommunications

The TOR may expect you to cover the home costs of telecommunications as part of either the backstopping services, or as covered by the overhead costs element of remuneration. Portable telephones are becoming an essential piece of equipment for field staff, and you should allow for at least two of these per project.

Document

In some projects this can form a substantial part of the project costs. The home office share of these costs may also be covered by the overhead costs element.

Staff administration

You should not assume that, if the TOR do not mention these costs, you will not have to pay them; or if you have a medical certificate of health for the key personnel from a doctor in your home country, that the authorities in the target country will accept it.

Translations

You will need translation and interpreting services during the course of the project, whether to translate the project reports and correspondence with the client, or whether to translate visa application requests, telephone bills, property rental statements and so on. The local support staff will be able to do much of the routine work, but will need assistance during crises.

Things which may go wrong

- The local authorities do not accept your staff's home country driving licences; they require your key personnel to take the local driving test, and someone fails it.

Summary: 11. Summary table
12. Contingencies

Description

Details for

- summary
  - all the previous ten elements of the financial costs
  - the local and base currencies
- contingencies.

Discussion

Summary

This should be a simple table showing the main cost headings (determined either by the TOR or by yourself) in terms of the local and the base currencies.

Contingencies

There are two types of unforeseen expenditure: those which arise during the project, and those which arise because you forgot to include something in the financial proposal. You should make some explicit allowance for the former in the proposal, and you may choose to make some hidden allowance for the latter.

Things which may go wrong

- Working with separate spreadsheets, you revise some of the detailed tables but forget to update the summary table. Use linked spreadsheets.

Appendices/other material

Description

Details for

- as required by the TOR
  - ○ copies of company certified accounts
  - ○ copies of salary statements for key staff
  - ○ profit forecasts for the next two years
  - ○ other certified documents.

Discussion

Some TOR require so many supporting documents that collecting or preparing them can be a full-time exercise of its own — particularly where they have to be originals, certified by a solicitor or notary public, and not less than (for example) three months old. Whether this information is particularly relevant is less important than the fact that the TOR ask you to provide them. Any omission could provide a bureaucratic reason to ignore the proposal altogether.

Where you have any questions on these documents, you should contact the client's project officer.

Things which may go wrong

- You do not read the TOR carefully enough, and overlook various papers which the TOR require you to provide.
- You mistakenly assume that certified documents are available on demand, and do not leave enough time to prepare them.
- You fail to resolve the conflict between the requirements of the TOR and your own country's laws on data protection.

Summary

The financial proposal is the most important of the written proposal documents, and you and your colleagues should take care to arrive at a reasonable estimate. It is worth noting that in doing so the greatest potential risk you run is not that the individual cost estimates are unsound, or that an element of expenditure has been overlooked, but that someone made a simple error in one of the spreadsheets.

Summary — writing financial proposals

- A bad technical proposal can cost you the project, but a bad financial proposal can cost you your company.
- 'Leaving it to the contract negotiations' means 'leaving it too late'.
- Save time and trouble by using pre-prepared modules and spreadsheets.
- It is more important that people check your calculations than your text.
- When developing a new worksheet (spreadsheet), compare the worksheet results against more than one hand-calculated answer from previously solved problems. Never trust a new worksheet.
- People will usually get the most complicated calculations right and the most simple things wrong.
- Don't bother to show costs to the nearest penny — even if you calculate them to the nearest penny.

8

Comparisons

Introduction

When you have finished the draft versions of the technical and financial proposals, one stage still stands between you and the post office: you cannot send off the documents until they have been checked. At least, this is the theory; in practice

- document comparison is one of the last steps in preparing international proposals
- it takes place when the proposals team is under the greatest pressure (Figs 7 and 8)
- and it is therefore an activity which is almost always cancelled.

This is a pity, since two days spent on comparing and reviewing the technical and financial proposals can lead to much more convincing final documents. The activity has three main parts: business comparison, a technical quality assurance check, and a style quality assurance check.

Business comparison

Your first reaction on completing the financial proposal might be that the total cost seems too high, and you may decide to reduce them. In some cases, the TOR will specify a limit for the project costs, and you may have to reduce your estimates. Yet you cannot change the financial proposal without changing the technical proposal (and vice-versa). For example, you may decide to

- *reduce the man – months* which means changes to the work programme and staffing schedule
- *select cheaper staff* which means changes to the CVs, and

perhaps to the association arrangements (if you decide to look for other JV partners with lower costs)

- *use lower-cost technology* which means changes to the approach and methodology
- *reduce the fee mark-up* which is the one possibility that does not affect the technical proposal, and so often the only one which the proposals team has left time for.

During the core period of work on the technical proposal, the team members may come up with new ways of carrying out some of the tasks, or they may discover improvements to the proposed work programme. These sensible changes to the technical proposal will have to be carried through to the financial proposal. The risk of not doing so is either that the client may not be impressed with your company's competence, or that he may accept your improved technical proposal and insist on paying the old, cheaper costs quoted in your financial proposal.

When you have revised the technical proposal you will need to check whether the changes you have made affect the financial proposal; if they do, and you do not like them, then you should return to the technical proposal and rethink the modifications you made there. Changes in one document will affect the other, and you will probably have to go round the loop (Fig. 15) a couple of times before you are satisfied that the two documents are consistent with each other.

Technical QA

Quality Assurance (QA) is one of the in-phrases of the 1990s, although in practice it often reduces to a mere form-filling procedure. In preparing proposals at least, it is an important, risk-avoidance process. In the technical QA check, an experienced engineer reads the proposal documents to make sure that they

- are internally consistent
- do not contain technical gaffes and errors
- make a convincing technical argument.

Style QA

While the technical QA checks the *contents* of the proposal documents, the style QA checks their *appearance*. For example, the different members of the JV group may supply text and other material in different font styles and sizes: your support staff should have imported the material into standard documents, but it is always

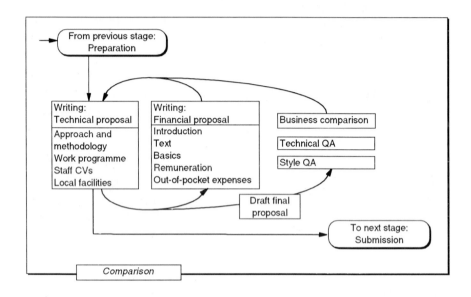

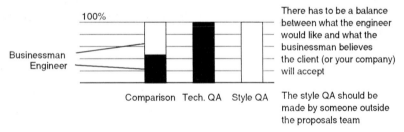

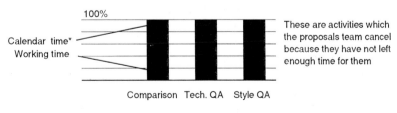

Fig. 15. Comparison and QA checks

possible that some differences remained. Important style QA checks include the

- correctly referenced table of contents
- page numbers
- page breaks
- headers and footers
- consistent styles throughout the proposal documents
- text.

The text check can be particularly important. If the client and reviewer cannot understand what you are trying to say they are unlikely to rate what you say very highly: the text must be readable and understandable. Few engineers can write this quality of text, and no-one can write it in a foreign language (people like Joseph Conrad are the exception, rather than the rule). Some companies even go to the trouble of employing outside staff to proofread their proposal document — people such as novelists or journalists, who can not only spot difficult text, but can also help improve it.

General

The benefit of QA checks is that they can spot errors and omissions in the original documents, while there is still time to correct them. There will always be errors of some sort to be found; this is one reason why publishing companies employ editors, and why newspapers employ proofreaders. Such checks can be very constructive.

Summary

- You will probably have to go round the loop a couple of times before you arrive at consistent, comparable technical and financial proposal documents.
- Comparison and QA checks are those important activities which the proposals team usually have no time left to carry out.
- The comparison checks should be made by members of the proposals team.
- The QA checks should *not* be made by members of the proposals team.
- The person making the technical QA check should be an experienced engineer.

9

Submission

Introduction

Submitting the documents should mean putting two copies into an
envelope and posting them off; but once again, life isn't that simple.
Each TOR will include a number of special instructions, ignoring
which can lose your company the project, however good your
proposal is (and however minor the special instructions). For example, the TOR can require you to

- put the technical and financial proposals into separate
  envelopes
- put the technical document into one envelope, seal it, add
  a message (such as 'not to be opened by the post department') and put it inside another envelope
- seal the envelope with sealing wax
- send copies of the proposal documents to various other
  people, besides the client
- stamp each document with the message 'original' or
  'copy', as appropriate
- submit the documents by a certain date.

The last one can cause the most inconvenience to the proposals team.
The submission phase of preparing a proposal also covers — besides
actually producing and dispatching the documents — clearing up
the proposals office, and allowing the proposals team to unwind.

Document production

There will probably be a copy-shop or other small business in your
area, which is prepared to produce any number of copies from the
original material which you send them. It may be worth having such
an outside firm produce the final documents for you, for a number
of reasons

- the outside firm may be able to make the copies more cheaply and quickly
- they may make fewer errors (at this point, the members of the proposal team will be running out of time, under considerable pressure, or both — and so are more likely to make silly mistakes)
- they may have better equipment (you can be sure that your own company's photocopier will break down when you need it most)
- they may be able to produce better quality copies (this particularly applies to colour plans and scanned colour photographs).

Whoever makes the copies, you will need to make sure that the original material is clearly laid out. Where the final document is fairly complicated — including a variety of divider sheets, page sizes and colour pages — you should also give the copier your master document. He then has a clear example to follow.

When the documents arrive back in your office, duly copied and bound, you should carry out a final edit check on them: it is not unknown for someone to miss out a page by mistake, or insert pages upside down. After doing this, you should prepare the documents for delivery, making sure that you observe any special requirements mentioned in the TOR.

Documents submission

Some advertisements for courier services may lead you to believe that a document can be sent to any part of the world, and arrive within 24 hours. In practice, you cannot even guarantee 24-hour delivery to somewhere in your own country; a practical estimate of delivery to other countries is one week or more. Most couriers will give you an estimate of the time it will take them to deliver the documents for you, but they will not normally guarantee delivery by a specified day. Although they may be 95% sure that they will actually deliver on the times they quote, bad weather or aircraft breakdowns can lead to missed connections and missed delivery times. For intercontinental deliveries you should be prepared to allow

- 1 day at your end of the shipment
- 1 day at the delivery end of the shipment
- 3 – 4 working days between each end
- 1 day for unforeseen emergencies.

You should certainly allow one day over the courier's estimates.

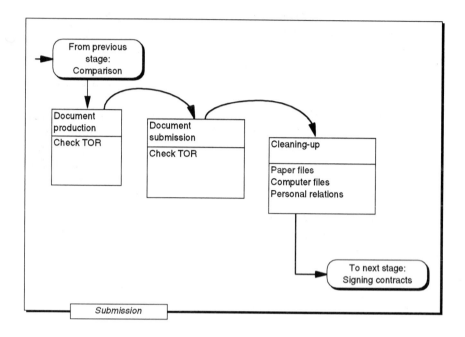

TASK INPUT

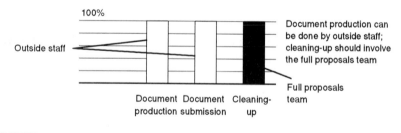

TIME INPUT

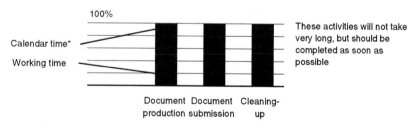

Fig. 16. Document submission

Cleaning up

As soon as the proposals documents have been posted off, you should set about clearing up the mess of paper and computer files which you have collected over the last several days. The tendency will be to put it off until later, but when later comes round you will have forgotten which are the latest files and which you can delete (etc.).

The reaction of the members of the proposals core team can fluctuate dramatically during the 24 hours after the documents were posted off — the post-proposal syndrome. Following the last few days of intense pressure, they can initially be exhilarated; but then morale and the quality of work can quickly fall to zero as a reaction sets in, and they will need to be left alone for a day to recover.

If you hope to keep the core team intact for work on future proposals, you should consider a small office celebration during this 24-hour period. It will serve as a means of

- defining the completion of a major piece of work
- thanking all the people who worked on the proposal
- cementing or repairing relations between them.

This is not the time to carry out a post-proposal examination of what went wrong (or right), and why.

Summary

- Answer the question: (Fig. 16) re-read the TOR to see what special requirements for the submission they may contain.
- Never assume 24-hour delivery.
- Allow at least one day over the courier's estimates for delivery time.
- Check that the copies contain the full number of pages, in the right order, and inserted the right way up.
- Allow the proposals core team a day to recover from the pressure.
- Get rid of 95% of the computer and paper files.
- Add one copy of the submitted documents to your company's proposal library.

10

Signing contracts

Preparation

If your proposal has been successful your company will probably be eager to visit the client and sign the contract. This eagerness should be resisted, on the grounds of 'fools rush in where angels fear to tread'. Usually you will want to discuss some of the details of the work with the client (which is why the proposal should include a section on comments on the TOR); and usually the client will want to discuss your price offer (and negotiate it downwards). Because of this, whoever does the negotiating must fully understand what you and your colleagues meant in the technical proposal, and what you costed for (and perhaps forgot to include) in the financial proposal. The negotiators should also have a good understanding of the future client and his representatives.

Negotiations

It can often be better to send a small negotiating team rather than an individual, given the range of questions which might arise. Nevertheless, negotiation is primarily a business skill rather than an engineering skill, and a specialist sub-section of business skills at that. You will also find that while most clients may not have as many engineering skills as your company, they will have very good negotiators. The best advice here is to employ an expert, or at least to read a wide range of specialist literature on the subject, attend training courses, and generally learn this specialist skill in advance of having to use it.

Bribery

Bribery is not part of any serious consultant's negotiating arsenal. Many international organisations are becoming more outspoken in denouncing it. James Wolfensohn, president of the World Bank, has been quoted as complaining of the 'cancer or corruption'[53] in poor countries. George Moody-Stuart, chairman of the UK chapter of Transparency International, says that today

> nobody in the business world pretends any more that (corruption) is not one of the most important and damaging factors in Third World development.[54]

He goes on to describe ways in which it occurs in international competitive bidding (ICB) and pre-qualification.

Safety nets

One weapon which should form part of your negotiating arsenal is a proposal for a contract safety net. Most contracts for international competitive bidding (ICB) are based to some extent on fair and reasonable behaviour (trust) between the client and the consultant. Sometimes this trust will break down, and both parties will need help in resolving their disagreement. The draft contract will probably include some method of arbitration, and of dispute resolution by resorting to law. You will need to make sure that these provisions are fair and reasonable to your company; your you may also want to include provision for mediation or adjudication experts or panels.

Signing contracts

If, after all the work you have put in — from initial marketing to preparing the detailed financial proposal — your company does sign a contract for the new project with the client, then congratulations!

Summary

(See Fig. 17)

- Make sure someone in the negotiating team has read and understood the technical proposal and both versions of the financial proposal.
- Send a team of people who know the client, know the technical work, and know how to negotiate business deals.

---

53 *Economist*, 5 October 1996, page 92.

54 *Time to take on corruption*, published in the New Civil Engineer, 19 September 1996.

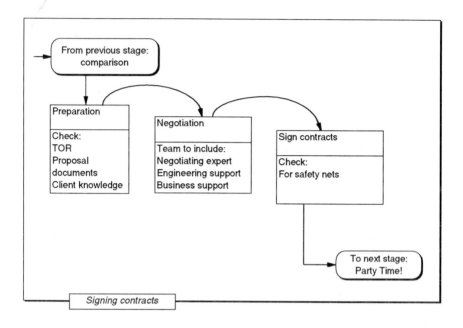

TASK INPUT

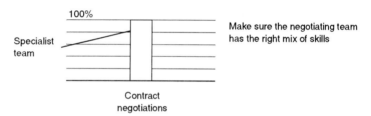

TIME INPUT

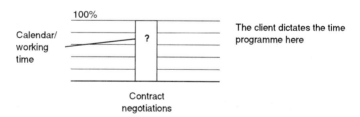

Fig. 17. Signing contracts

- Sending the average engineer to lead final negotiations can be like giving a loaded gun to a four-year old: someone is going to get hurt (and it won't be the client).
- Make sure the safety net provided for in the draft contract is not one-sided.

11

Follow-up/Marketing (2)

Whatever happens, whether you win or lose this particular project, business life will go on. You will have to start all over again and look for another interesting new project to compete for. Before you do so, you might want to discuss with your colleagues just how important the technical proposal is in project acquisition.

Importance of the technical proposal: the programme in perspective

The technical proposal, considered alone, is extremely important, and should be as good as you can afford (in money and time) to make it. In the overall area of project acquisition, however, it is rather unimportant: it is just one of a number of links in the chain of events which lead from initial marketing to signing the contract.

Comparative Importance of the Technical Proposal Figure 18 shows a subjective estimate of the relative importance of some of the links in this chain.

- *marketing* is more important than the technical proposal; if people dislike the idea of buying goods from a stranger, they will never award expensive contracts to a completely unknown consultant (however good the technical proposal)
- *PQs* and the other formal steps in consultant selection are more important than the technical proposal: if you submit a poor PQ you won't even be on the shortlist to submit a technical proposal
- the *financial proposal* is more important than the technical proposal: a poor technical proposal can lose you the project, a poor financial proposal can lose you your company (if it goes bankrupt)

- *other unquantifiables* play a part in the client's decision on who to award the contract to: he is not necessarily obliged to award it to the best technical proposal submitted, or the lowest financial proposal. Such unquantifiables include political and business influences, for example

  - ○ the client wants a spread of countries in the pool of consultants to whom he awards projects
  - ○ the client's evaluators studied in a particular country and have a bias towards it as a result
  - ○ the client wants to add another company to his pool of preferred consultants.

As a result of the above points, the (subjective) percentages in Fig. 18 suggest that the technical proposal accounts for only 15% of the activity involved in project acquisition.

Comparative time spent on the technical proposal Figure 19 shows a subjective estimate of the relative time spent on some of the links in this chain

- *marketing* takes much more time than the technical proposal; it is in fact one activity which should be going on all the time
- good *preparation* can take as much time as the technical proposal, simply because it can save time on the technical proposal
- the *financial proposal* should take at least as much time as the technical proposal, because it is even more important.

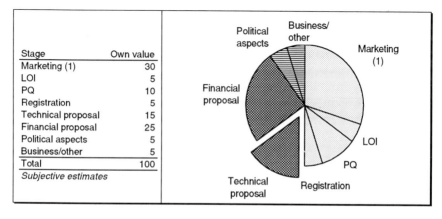

Stage	Own value
Marketing (1)	30
LOI	5
PQ	10
Registration	5
Technical proposal	15
Financial proposal	25
Political aspects	5
Business/other	5
Total	100
Subjective estimates	

Fig. 18. *Importance of the technical proposal*

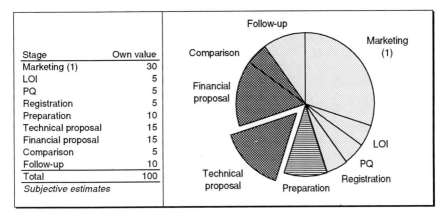

Stage	Own value
Marketing (1)	30
LOI	5
PQ	5
Registration	5
Preparation	10
Technical proposal	15
Financial proposal	15
Comparison	5
Follow-up	10
Total	100
Subjective estimates	

Fig. 19. Comparative time spent on the technical proposal

The (subjective) percentages in Fig. 19 suggest that the technical proposal accounts for only 15% of the time spent in project acquisition.

Follow-up

Win or lose, you should follow-up submission of your proposal with a visit to the potential client. Where a bank is involved in reviewing the proposal documents, you should visit your contacts there as well. One purpose of these visits is to find out where your proposals were strong and where they were poor. The information will help you to make improvements in your next submission. You should also try to get sight of the proposals submitted by your competitors, to see how they compare with your own. Just as important, you should use the follow-up visits to reassure the client that, even if you may not have won this project, you are still interested in working for his organisation. The visits then become part of the normal, contact-refreshment aspect of marketing.

At this time you should also organise a round-table discussion with the other members of the proposals team. They will have had time to recover from the stress of working on the proposals, but not yet time to forget the problems that arose. This post-proposal examination should identify improvements in your internal organisation, in the proposals work programme, and so on.

After both these steps, and to close down the proposal, you should write an informal, post-submission report, to serve as a future reference for yourself and other people who lead proposals activities.

Marketing (2)

With the lessons learnt during your work on the proposals, and during your follow-up meetings and discussions, you may well want to revise your marketing strategy. Perhaps you have identified weaknesses in your company's organisation which mean that you cannot emphasise the technical products that you had tried to sell; perhaps some regions of the world have proved to be particularly difficult or expensive for your company to work in; or perhaps the client has proved to be unreasonable and over-demanding. Your company should also take the opportunity to review its project identification and selection procedures.

Summary

- If you did not win, analyse the reasons, learn from your experience, and modify your approach accordingly for your next tender. And do tender again. You have to compete in order to win.[55]
- Review and revise your company's marketing strategy.
- Review and revise your proposals programme and resources.
- Whether you win or lose the contract, visit the client again.
- Learn from your experience.
- A well-prepared but unsuccessful proposal can lead to more work than a badly-prepared but successful one.

---

55 EBRD *Guide to procurement opportunities* 1993, page 14. The other tips on winning on this page are also well worth thinking over.

12

References

Consulting companies sell advice. The only ways they have of demonstrating that they can sell good advice is to describe

- the projects which they carried out in the past — their proven track record
- the skills and experience of the professional staff who work for them today.

These two types of evidence are the project references and the staff references, or staff CVs (CV is short for the Latin term *curriculum vitae*; it is about time that someone invented an English phrase to replace it, possibly one which is more attractive than the American–English *biodata*). Your company's first priority should be to make sure that its pool of project and staff references is up-to-date, since it will provide more supporting material for all your marketing activities, from promotional literature through EOIs and PQs to proposals. For each 1% deficiency in the pool of references you will probably lose 1% of your chances of winning a new project — before you even start trying.

Project references

Types Project references come in a number of shapes and sizes, partly because many banks have their own idiosyncracies and preferences when it comes to their layout and content, but also because you will have different uses for them. In order of increasing size, the main types are

- *Project lists*: when preparing brochures or proposals, you will want to refer to those projects which most closely meet the requirements of the document, perhaps because they were for similar types of work or were carried out in the same part of the world. To provide a suitable mix of sectoral and regional projects, you will need some idea of almost every project which your company has been involved in. This does not mean that the source project list must give full details of every project; but it should at least include

- ○ the project title, location and technical sector
- ○ projects less than ten years old, and worth more than (e.g.) a fee of US$ 20 000.

This briefest form of project reference will include minimum details of perhaps 80% of all your firm's projects.

- *Short references*: these are the most common ammunition for marketing-related documents. They extend the basic information of the project lists by adding a brief paragraph of text describing the overall project, and highlighting the most interesting aspects of the services that your company provided for it. For inclusion in documents, short references are best presented in the form of a table — and with the page orientation the same as the rest of the document text. There is nothing to be gained and much to be lost (in terms of annoyance) in expecting the reader to turn a document round 90 degrees every page or two. For the more complex projects you may want to prepare a number of different short references — one to emphasise the project management services your company provided, and others to describe the engineering supervision services, the highway design services, and so on. Short references in a table layout should not take up more than the equivalent of ten or so lines of text. You should eventually build up a reserve of short references for perhaps 60% of all your firm's projects.
- *Medium references* are a half-way house between the short and long project references. They give you the chance to describe in some detail the nature of the project, all the various services your company provided, and the problems which it overcame in the process. This type of reference is mainly targetted at readers who are skilled engineers, and can be useful for project descriptions in PQs. Medium project references may prove useful for perhaps 40% of all your firm's projects.

- *Long references* provide full information about the project, including details of the client and of other companies associated in providing the services for it. They are useful for very detailed PQs, and for proposals. A good example of a layout for this sort of reference is the form the ADB specify in its TOR. Long project references may prove useful for perhaps 20–40% of all your firm's projects.
- *PR references* are colourfully-presented project descriptions for use in publicity brochures and other public relations (PR) material. Some companies also insist on including them in proposal documents, whatever the TOR specify to the contrary. Here the emphasis is on an eye-catching layout, with one or more colour photographs or plans accompanied by a few brief paragraphs of text. PR references may be appropriate for 10–20% of your firm's projects.
- *Client-defined references*: whatever reference material you may have prepared in advance, you should not be surprised to find that each TOR asks you to provide something different either in terms of the layout or content. By definition, you will not be able to prepare exactly these references in advance.

Staff references (CVs)

Types Staff and project references have much in common, both in their types, contents and in their preparation. For example, staff references also come in a number of shapes and sizes — and as with project references, because you will have different uses for them.

- *Staff lists*: one of the first things you will need to do in preparing a proposal is to check whether your company has the all the specialist staff needed to carry it out. The staff lists will help you do so. They should contain basic information about the professional staff in your company, including staff name, qualifications, and what regions and sectors he/she has experience in. This briefest form of staff reference should include minimum details of all your firm's professional personnel.
- *Short CVs* presented in table format: they briefly describe the educational qualifications and more important (i.e. most relevant) experience of the staff concerned. They are the key summaries of each member of staff. You will eventually build up a reserve of short references for perhaps 80% of all your firm's professional personnel.

(Remember, the professional staff and their expertise are the only thing that your company has to sell.)

- *Medium CVs* combine a summary of the individual's personal details (age, nationality etc.) with a list of his professional qualifications and a brief resume of his professional experience. They should not take more than a page of text, and are best suited as ready-use material for EOIs and PQs, particularly where time is short. Medium CVs will also prove useful for at least 60% or so of all your firm's professional staff.

- *Long CVs* provide full information about the staff concerned, including details (such as size or cost) of the more important projects on which they have worked. They are essential for proposals, and important sources of material for the various other types of staff CV (since it is easier to create a summary CV from a detailed one than it is to create a detailed CV from a summary). You are most likely to be able to sell the services of staff with the most experience and qualifications, and so should concentrate on preparing long CVs for these people (who may be no more than 20% of your firm's professional personnel) who have

  - a professional degree
  - at least five years professional experience
  - already worked overseas.

- *Public relation CVs* combine a paragraph describing the expert's key qualifications with a note on his position in the company and, often, a photograph (use of photographs is of questionable value; if a professional photographer is not used the results can give the reader the impression that the person shown is either unpleasant, a fool, or both). Public relation CVs may be appropriate for less than 20% of your firm's personnel.

- *Client-defined CVs*: as with project references, you should not be surprised to find that each TOR asks you to provide CVs in a different layout or with different contents.

Development of references

Your company will probably already have available a supply of various types of project reference. This does not mean that they cover the most interesting projects and personnel, or that they accurately describe the project and the services your firm provided. Unless your company has some sort of Quality Assurance manual, and applied this to the preparation of references (which would be unusual) you should treat the quality of any available material with a degree of scepticism. To refresh your firm's references you should

- *collect available base material*: In a crisis you have to use what is already available, and you should at least know where it is.
- *define a storage and retrieval system*: In most companies, several people will be interested in using reference material, and so you will have to develop a system for storing it (and for other people to find it). Initially you may want to use a simple system of text files and paper storage, but you should eventually consider storing and retrieving references from a database. As the final product will be paper-based forms, you should design these forms before you design the database.
- *check the style QA*: The available base material may have been prepared by various departments of your company, and so may appear in different layouts. The next step is for you to bring them all into a uniform style.
- *check the technical QA*: As time becomes available you will then have to make sure that the information you have in the base material is in fact both correct and complete. This will prove most difficult with CVs. You will be surprised at the inability of most engineers to prepare a decent CV for themselves, let alone for other people. But even checking project references can cause headaches, if different people give a different meaning to some of the information requested. For example, is the start date of a project the date the contract was signed or the date work started on site; and is the end date of a particular project the date the work was handed over to the client, the date of payment of retention money, or the end of the maintenance period. You may need to prepare a set of definitions to ensure the consistency of both the technical QA checks and the supply of new material.
- *collect new material*: Eventually you will have time to collect information on other projects and staff currently missing from your base material. The biggest problems you will have here is convincing your management that it will be time well-spent, and squeezing the relevant information out of your firm's technical departments.

Contents Tables 38, 39 and 40 together with Figs 20 and 21 give an idea of what should be included in each type of project reference and CV.

Improving references

However many project references and staff CVs you prepare, there will never be enough to exactly match the requirements of every project your company is interested in. The question then arises as to how much (if at all) you should modify the most suitable references which you do have available.

Project references   To some extent, modification and improvement is entirely reasonable. For example, your company may have designed a major new road project. In one case you might want to emphasise the difficult soil conditions which your company had to allow for, while in another case the careful environmental protection measures your firm designed might be more relevant. Both accurately describe the services provided, but from different angles. Alternatively, adding details of associated bridge design works (which were actually carried out by another consultant) would be going a step too far. One reason for this is self-preservation. Once you have issued a project reference, whether in PR material or in a proposal, you are put on the spot in two ways

(*a*)   it will be difficult to change it in any material way, without giving the impression of fabrication of evidence
(*b*)   it will be read by other companies who worked with yours on the project, and who will be happy to point out errors in your references, should they ever be competing with your company for an important new project.

Table 38.   Key backstopping points

Key qualifications of backstopping staff*
Has worked in the project country
Has several years working experience
Is a qualified engineer in at least one aspect of the project
Has met the client
Has good connections inside the consulting firm
Is at least at the level of middle-management in the firm
Has good connections in other firms associated in the project

Backstopping tasks*
Reassuring the site staff
Reassuring the client
Solving personal problems of the site staff
Solving business problems
Solving technical problems

* In order of priority.

Table 39.   Contents of project references

Contents	Short	Medium	Long	PR	Lists
Company details	Not needed — covered by other material				
Project details					
Project name	✔	✔	✔	✔	✔
Project reference number	–	–	–	–	✔
Country/location (geographical sector)	✔	✔	✔	✔	✔
Technical sector	✔	✔	✔	✔	✔
Year of completion	✔	✔	✔	✔	✔
Work period (from–to), giving year and month	✔	✔	✔	–	–
Size/length	✔	✔	✔	✔	–
Short description (project, own services)	✔	–	–	✔	–
Expanded description (project, own services)	–	✔	✔	–	–
Full description (project, own services, problems)	–	✔	✔	–	–
Total contract value	–	–	✔	✔	✔
Client details					
Client name	✔	✔	✔	✔	–
Client's project reference number	–	–	–	–	✔
Client address	–	–	✔	–	–
Client contact	–	–	✔	–	–
Your company's input					
Associated firms	–	✔	✔	–	–
Prime consultant or associate firm	–	–	✔	–	–
Man–months input from your company	–	✔	✔	–	–
Man–months input from other companies	–	–	✔	–	–
Value of services provided by your company	✔	✔	✔	✔	✔
Project costs and fees					
Total project cost	✔	✔	✔	✔	–
Consultants fees	–	–	✔	–	✔

Notes. Make sure that you and your colleagues agree on what each of these items actually means.

Staff CVs   Similar arguments can be made for staff CVs. If you want to fully describe the professional experience of someone who has been working as an engineer for more than ten years then you could probably write enough to fill a book. Every CV is a career summary; some just summarise more than others. Take the example of someone who worked as resident engineer, supervising the construction of a section of new motorway. He may have supervised the work from

Table 40. Contents of staff references

Contents	Short	Medium	Long	PR	Lists
Personal details					
Name	✔	✔	✔	✔	✔
Nationality	✔	✔	✔	✔	–
Date of birth	✔	✔	✔	–	–
Married status	–	–	–	–	✔
Photograph	–	–	–	✔	–
Profession	✔	✔	✔	✔	✔
Position in present company	✔	✔	✔	✔	–
Years with present company	–	✔	✔	✔	–
Educational qualifications	–	✔	✔	✔	✔
Post-graduation training	–	✔	✔	–	–
Membership of professional bodies	–	✔	✔	–	–
Publications	–	✔	✔	✔	–
Language skills	–	✔	✔	–	✔
Years of professional experience	✔	✔	✔	–	✔
Key qualifications (region, sector experience)	✔	✔	✔	–	–
Project details					
Project name	–	✔	✔	–	–
Country/location (geographical sector)	–	✔	✔	–	
Technical sector	–	✔	✔	–	–
Year of completion	–	✔	✔	–	–
Work period (from — to)	–	✔	✔	–	–
Size/length	–	✔	✔	–	–
Short description (project, own services)	–	✔	–	–	–
Expanded description (project, own services)	–	–	✔	–	–
Full description (project, own services, problems)	–	–	–	–	–
Client details (=previous employers)					
Client name	✔	✔	✔	–	–
Client address	–	–	–	–	–
Client contact	–	–	–	–	–
Staff member's own input	Not needed — covered by project details				
Project costs and fees					
Total project cost	–	✔	✔	–	–
Consultants fees	–	–	–	–	–

initial site clearance through to the end of the maintenance period. For one proposal you may want to emphasise his experience in the supervision of earthworks, for another proposal perhaps his work with asphaltic road surfacing material will be more important. Such changes are legitimate improvements of the starter CV, although you should check with the owner of the CV for accuracy.

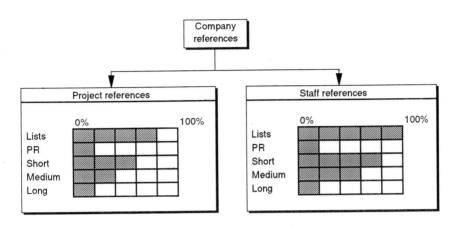

Fig. 20.   References

In a perfect world, the best way to prepare a CV would be to ask the owner to do it himself — after, of course, giving him an example of a good CV (with the layout you or the client have defined, properly completed). Most of the staff references prepared in this way will be unusable, either because they are too thin, or too exaggerated. For example, where one engineer describes his professional career of thirty years as

>   1960–1990: employed as highway engineer

then the occasional CV can almost suggest that the engineer managed to compress the equivalent of ten full-time careers into an afternoon's work, e.g.

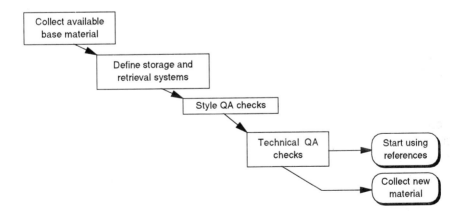

Fig. 21.   Development of references

> 1990–1991: assistant resident engineer on a 30 km section of new motorway construction in southern England. Duties included supervision of earthworks, approval of post-tensioning operations on several bridge projects, redesign of road pavement, negotiations with client, and supervision of final maintenance and other corrective works. Also headed the company's regional office in China.

Such CVs are not likely to impress the informed reviewer. For 90% of the CVs which you want to collect, you will have to interview their owners directly, and prepare their CVs for them.

Other types of reference

Backstopping When the Apollo 13 astronauts had problems, a million miles from home, they were not entirely alone: they could still communicate with the base, for both moral support and technical advice. When you buy a new computer from one of the better suppliers, you know that someone will be available at the end of a telephone help-line, should you get into difficulties with it. Both cases are examples of backstopping, and it is surprising how universal a practice it is, once you start looking for it.

Backstopping is the art of providing reassurance, advice and technical support to someone who is physically remote from the reassurer. It can never be provided by people who have not directly experienced similar problems themselves (which is why the NASA team includes former astronauts) and who do not understand the technical difficulties surrounding the problem (which is why the computer help-line is staffed by people who know the mechanics of the equipment they sold you). Banks and their clients typically place enormous weight on the personnel selected for the project team, and comparatively little on the backstopping service which the consulting company can also offer. This almost suggests that someone can set up a shell company with two permanent staff and a register of freelancers, and then compete on an equal basis with a company which has a large pool of experienced, international project engineers.

Most PC-magazines would advise you to stay away from sellers of computers who do not provide a decent backup service. Clients of consulting companies should take the same attitude. They should arguably place a substantial proportion of their evaluation points (perhaps 10%) on the consultant's competence in providing backstopping services.

Client lists Nothing convinces a potential customer more than references from previous, satisfied customers. You should consider preparing a list of such customers of your firm, and including it in marketing material such as EOI, PQ and general company brochures. The list should be sorted by region and type of customer, so that the prospective client can identify organisations similar to his own. You should also make sure that your previous clients have no objection to being mentioned in your list.

Summary

- The first priority for the marketing department of a consulting company is to check their supply of project and staff references.
- If you plan to set up a database for project references, define the information you want in the references before you design the database.
- In improving project references and staff CVs, don't exaggerate.
- You should always check with the owner of a CV for accuracy, if you decide to beautify it.
- Don't expect that most of your colleagues will be able to prepare their own CVs by themselves: they won't.
- Develop a backstopping centre of excellence.
- Prepare a list of satisfied clients.
- You may want to avoid preparing long or PR project references for work which left the client (rightly or wrongly) dissatisfied.

13

Discussion

Clients' desire for complicated bid documents for the more reward-
ing new projects is likely to continue for the foreseeable future. The
chances are also that the documents will become more expensive to
produce, rather than less. One reason may be that there are many
more internationally active consulting companies, competing for
fewer (if larger) new projects. The whole exercise suggests a certain
short-sightedness on the part of the international financing agencies,
since in the end it is the client who pays the costs of all proposals
(successful and unsuccessful). More, companies may have to concentrate their best staff on writing proposals, and leave the second
rank to actually carry out the project.

The present system has problems of its own. For example, both
consultants and clients can operate in a less than efficient and
competent manner — and occasionally do so. Everyone would benefit from an open debate between all parties; an understanding of each
others' problems would go some way to finding solutions for them.
This is not something which a single consultant or bank can under-
take, however. For the purposes of this debate, the following notes
suggest some of the problems which clients have with consultants,
and which consultants have with clients (limited of course to various
aspects of international proposals).

What clients dislike about consultants

Registrations Consultants who do not produce all the information
requested in the registration forms; and consultants who produce
incorrect information.

Marketing Consultants who make too many marketing visits; who
make too few marketing visits; who change their marketing representative every month. Consultants whose marketing representatives

do not know (technically) what they are talking about; who do not know the difficulties (technical and political) of the client's country.

EOI and PQ EOI and PQ which are too long; which do not supply the information requested.

TOR Consultants who do not read (and respond to) the TOR.

Technical proposals Consultants who submit CVs of excellent staff, and then fail to provide them for the project (or who try to replace them a month or so after they have been on site). Consultants who copy text wholesale from textbooks; who provide superficially pretty work programmes but ones which in detail do not match the accompanying staffing programmes or cost estimates.

Proposal documents Documents which are poorly presented and difficult to understand; which do not provide the information requested in the TOR, or not in the order prescribed in the TOR; which do not provide the services requested in the TOR. Documents which are not delivered on time (although this probably disturbs the consultants more than it does the client).

Project references Consultants who exaggerate or fabricate details in their project references, for example claiming as their own work, something which was carried out by another consultant or sub-consultant. These consultants should be reported to FIDIC, and their names eventually added to an annually published list of the best (and worst) responding consultants.

CVs Consultants who over-exaggerate details of a person's professional experience. One result can be that the selected site staff cannot actually do the work. CV's which are too long; too short; not in the specified layout; which are exaggerated; which are not signed as requested. Consultants who propose the same staff in two different proposals in which the projects will take place at the same time.

What consultants dislike about clients

Shortlists Clients who do not have the energy to produce a shortlist of five or six companies, but invite as many as 14 to submit proposals; their names should be added to an annually published list of the best (and worst) responding consultants.

Registrations Clients who produce over-complicated registration systems (so that the consultant cannot even understand what information the client is asking for, let alone provide it). Clients who produce registration systems which define complicated and poorly understood lists of technical sectors; which do not define sectors for new products; which request the same information but in different ways (e.g. both paper and diskette-based); whose diskette-based system is not user-friendly or is based on out-of-date software technology.

TOR Clients who change the TOR after they have been issued: this simply increases the cost of all the consultants' bids. Clients who do so should pay each consultant for the extra work; alternatively, they should be reported to an international panel of (e.g.) FIDIC and World Bank appointees, whose task is to improve the system. Clients who prepare TOR which are too detailed or which penalise consultants who include qualifications, reservations or clarifications in them

> too rigorous rules sometimes limit necessary flexibility and often do not achieve the desired result to ensure equal treatment.[56]

Proposal documents Clients who cancel the project after calling for (and receiving) the proposals; they should be obliged to pay the consultants for their abortive work.

Financial proposals Clients who ask for too much financial information; providing enough information to be able to estimate staff rates is reasonable, providing information on the breakdown of overhead costs and social charges is not reasonable. Someone buys a chair based on its design and its total cost — he doesn't ask to see the cost of the chair-covering fabric before making a decision. Clients who try to place restrictions on how much consultants may pay their staff (or whether e.g. the consultant may pay his staff an overseas allowance); that is surely a matter for the consultant and his staff alone.

Negotiations Clients who break the rules: in a two-envelope system, by opening the financial proposals first.

---

56 Agne Sandberg, in a paper on competitive tendering or negotiation in the 3rd World Bank/FIDIC Conference on International Procurement, 1996 (pub. *Civil Engineer International*).

CVs Clients who insist on signatures on staff CVs at the proposals stage, where time pressures are great. It should be more than sufficient to ask for signed CVs at the contract negotiation stage. Clients who place too much emphasis on the perfect CV; someone who can be a good theoretical engineer in his home country can be very poor at adapting to the problems of living and working in a foreign country. Clients who insist that the proposed staff sign to say they will be available for their project, even though the proposal has only a 1 in 6 chance of succeeding (and the persons concerned need a 1 in 1 chance of finding themselves new work for the future).

Negotiations Clients who place too little emphasis on quality and too much on price.

14

Summary

This book will help you to write a good proposal; and it will help you to argue for the resources you need to do it. What it will not do is provide you with all the knowledge you need for each specific proposal you will become involved in. In particular, you will need to invest time and effort in reading about the financing agencies, and about the geography and society of the country you are interested in. These are not specifically engineering subjects, but are just as important to a successful proposal.

The following notes list the most important points to remember in preparing international proposals; and describe some of the problems which can arise in preparing proposals and working on international projects. If you now have to write a proposal of your own, then I wish you good luck.

Important points to remember

- Be prepared for problems: Murphy's Law applies just as much to the preparation of proposals as it does to most other forms of engineering.
- *Presentation* of the proposal is more important than the detailed *work programme* for the project, which is more important than the *financial proposal*, which is more important than the rest of the *technical proposal*.
- It's better to submit an *imperfect* proposal on time rather than a *perfect* proposal two days late.
- Prepare a work programme for the proposal, and work to it.
- Start with the draft technical proposal before the financial proposal.
- Selecting and preparing the CVs will always be a critical path activity.

- Keep a core team of people (*not* exclusively engineers) with experience in writing and preparing international proposals.
- In any proposal or related document (e.g. PQs), *answer the question.*
- Coming first in the proposals evaluation does not mean that your company has won the project, just as *not* coming in first means that your company has lost it.
- Include local knowledge in the text of the proposal.
- Never underestimate the client.
- Don't try for 100% quality — you can't afford it.
- To win a project you have to write a proposal; to write a proposal you must first be asked to submit one; and to be invited, the client first has to know your company exists.
- Try to find out what the client really wants, as opposed to what the TOR says he wants.

Things that go wrong with proposals (and projects)

In proposals

- It takes six weeks for your company to decide whether to submit a proposal, leaving you one week to prepare and write it (and a week to submit it).
- You discover that your contacts in your partner companies know even less about preparing an international proposal than you do.
- The CVs are not ready on time (this always happens).
- You find a printing error in one of the documents just as the secretary is wrapping them up for the courier (this also always happens).
- You forgot to include public holidays in your proposals programme and so lose contact with the local office for a week (*or*, the submission date is the 31st December).
- You discover that it will take four weeks to arrange a visa for the site visit.
- Someone binds the proposals documents with pages inserted upside-down or missing completely (this always happens).
- One of the proposed key personnel withdraws two days before you post the proposal documents.
- Bad weather delays the courier flight.
- The client changes the TOR during the programme period.
- The client cancels the project.

- The person making the site visit forgets to ask all the questions you gave him.
- To deliver the document on time, you have to wake up the caretaker of the client's office building at five minutes to midnight on the day of submission of the document.

In projects

- Staff are shown off the site at gunpoint by protestors.
- The client has not completed purchase of the project site.
- Two government departments sign separate works on the same site which are to be carried out at the same time.
- Your project does not have all the necessary clearances from involved government departments.
- Project staff are kidnapped.
- One of the selected site staff fails the local driving test.
- A project member is arrested for smoking a cigarette in public during Ramadan (an example of ignorance of, or lack of respect for, correct local behaviour).
- Returning from leave, one of the site team boards the wrong plane and is interned for three weeks in Russia.
- A member of the project team is killed in a local road accident.
- Another member of the project team elopes with someone else's wife.
- Yet another member of the team goes absent without leave at the end of a vacation period.

15

Check lists

The following pages give some examples of useful check lists for people who have to work on international proposals. They are not necessarily exhaustive — you will be able to think of further check lists of your own, and will probably want to change or add fields to these examples. The lists cover

- consultants' own project selection procedures (1)
- proposals team (2)
- site visit questions (3)
- technical proposals — basic details (4)
- structure and content of the technical proposal (5)
- items covered by the financial proposal level — remuneration (6)
- items covered by the financial proposal level — out-of-pocket expenses (a) (7)
- items covered by the financial proposal level — out-of-pocket expenses (b) (8)
- structure and content of the financial proposal (9)
- notes for people working overseas for the first time (10)
- contents of project references (11)
- contents of staff references

Check list 1. Consultants' own project selection procedures

Level 1 — Selection

General	Details	Notes
Background	Does the project match your strategy? Can you do the project? Can you make money from the project? Do you have contacts to support you?	*(One negative answer and forget it)*

Level 2 — Selection

General	Detail	Notes
Background	Project name Location Value Client Funding agency	
Practical	What are the chances of winning the project? Has the deadline for submitting an EOI passed? Is the project well financed? Is there time to write a good proposal? Is there staff to write a good proposal?	Check with your contacts
Business	Do you need to associate with other firms? What are your costs likely to be? What are your profits likely to be? What other advantages are there?	Doing so will reduce profits Apart from financial profit
Technical	Do you have good project references? Do you have enough good specialist staff?	If not, look for a JV partner Look for JV firm/ freelancers
Decision	Decide to continue or to drop this project. If to continue, what priority do you give it and what are the deadlines?	e.g. LOI submission date

Note. It does not matter whether you select the projects which are most interesting by using some sort of a checklist, by using a numbers-based evaluation chart, or by simply discussing possibilities with someone over a cup of coffee. It does matter that you should have *some sort* of project selection procedure.

Check list 2. Proposals team

Team	Team member	Main tasks	Check ✔
Core team	Team leader Technical writer General support Graphics support Country expert		
Specialists	Technical experts Businessman Management support Project management expert Accountant		
Short-term support	Legal advisor Translator VIP Technical QA Style QA		
Company links	Representatives in partner companies		
Proposals office	Standard computer hardware/software Proposals library Spare desk and computer Wall maps Laying out tables Tea and coffee facilities		
Proposals budget			
Proposals programme			

Check list 3. Site visit questions

General	Detail	Check ✔
Contacts Client	Who is the client's lead contact? Who will be *evaluating* the proposals? Who will be *deciding* on the proposals? Obtain organisation and staffing chart	
Funding agency	Which is the funding agency? Who is agency's project officer? Who in the agency is the decision-maker? Obtain organisation and staffing chart	
Local partner Other	Networking with local partner's staff List all *'concerned'* government officials List all *'concerned'* local organisations Provide an organisations boundary plan Identify contact in your local embassy	
Project details	Obtain location plan Reports referred to or listed in the TOR Details of local design standards Details of local materials Summarise project details Copies of other relevant technical material Details of other nearby current or proposed projects Details of any environmental/ resettlement studies	
Background	Details of project history and politics What computer hardware/software does the client use? Details of local climate, society Actually visit the project site Take site photographs	
Business	Find out what the client really wants (cf what the TOR says) What does the client think is particularly important? What extras would the client like? Identify potential local partners VIP meeting to impress the client with your interest in the work	
Financial	Identify local costs (accommodation, transport, support staff etc)	

Check list 4. Technical proposals — basic details

General	Detail	Notes	Check ✔
Techniques	Copying text? Use of modules? Technology-based approach? Task-based approach?		
Administration	Master copy Project diary Contacts address file Paper/computer file system		
Style notes	Page size and orientation Page headers and footers Page numbering Text style List colour pages Type of binder Type of divider sheet		

Check list 5. Structure and content of the technical proposal

Main section	Typical contents	
1. Title page, edge page	Title page, edge page	
2. Submission letter	Statement of intent	Contact names and details
3. Table of contents	Table of contents List of tables	List of figures
4. Introduction	Structure of the document	Executive summary
	Introduction to the company(s)	Location plan
5. Company description and experience *including sub-consultants*	Description of the company(s) Company organisation Company experience Company project references	Company regional experience Company current work load Company backstopping ability
6. Site appreciation	Site photographs Client technical meetings	
7. Project appreciation	Master schedule/master plan Project objectives	
8. Approach and methodology (1) task lists	Task lists	

Main section	Typical contents	
9. Approach and methodology (2) technical notes	Approach and methodology	Optional services
	Alternative concepts	Project management methods
	Additional services	Task list
10. Approach and methodology (3) key themes	Environmental monitoring	Training/technology transfer notes
	Resettlement monitoring	Computer hardware and software
	Project management	Backstopping methods/ means
	Support for minorities	Quality Assurance
11. Work programme	Organisation chart	Staffing schedules
	Critical path chart	Man – month estimates
	Work programme	Key personnel tasks
12. Comments on the TOR		
13. Staff CVs	List of key personnel	Backstopping CV
	Key personnel CVs	List of technical support staff
	Signatures for the CVs	CVs summary table
14. Association arrangements	Association agreements	Signed copy of other documents
	Initialled copy of the TOR	
15. Estimates of local facilities	Local staff	Local accommodation
	Local transport	Local equipment
16. Appendices/other material	Site visit photographs	= possibly useful
	Company brochures	= not recommended
	List of abbreviations	= often useful
	List of definitions	= sometimes useful

Notes. This check list is copied from Table 27 in chapter 6.

Check list 6. Items covered by the financial proposal

Level 1 — Remuneration

Level 2	Level 3	Level 4,5 Costs =	Foreign	Local
Basic salaries	International staff	Key personnel Backstoppers		
	Local staff	Local key staff *engineers* *sociologists* *environmental* *sociologists*		
	Local staff	Technical support *laboratory* *technicians* *survey assistants* *traffic interviewers* *draughstmen* *translators* *interpreters*		
	Local staff	Non-technical support *secretaries/typists* *receptionists* *drivers* *guards* *tea-boys, messengers*		
Social charges	Leave	Statutory holidays Vacation leave Sick leave Emergency leave Local public holidays Religious holidays		
	Financial benefits	Bonus/incentive 13th month pay Company/car loan Meal allowances		
	Social expenses	Social security contributions		

Level 2	Level 3	Level 4,5 Costs =	Foreign	Local
		Health and medical expenses		
		Retirement/ superannuation		
	Miscellaneous	Education/training benefits		
Overhead costs	Buildings, equipment	Rent		
		Depreciation expense		
		Amortisation expense		
		Utilities		
		Repairs and maintenance		
		Office furnishings and equipment		
	Consumables	Data processing		
		Office supplies, printing		
		Communication and postage		
	Non-billable staff	Administration staff		
		Partners		
		International representatives		
	Professional costs	Professional fees		
		Research and development		
		Professional training		
	Miscellaneous	Advertising and promotions		
		Travel and transportation		
		Taxes, licences, permits		
		Insurances		
Fee mark-up	Fees and profit			

Check list 7.   Items covered by the financial proposal

Level 1 — Out-of-pocket expenses (a)

Level 2	Level 3	Level 4,5 Costs =	Foreign	Local
Per diem	Travel per diem	International staff Local staff		
	Residential per diem	International staff Local staff		
	Other	Bonus Overseas allowance Housing allowance Education allowance		
Transport	International (air)	International staff International staff (families) Local staff Contract start/ leave travel Airport taxes		
	Equipment	Air freight Surface freight		
	Personal luggage	Accompanied Unaccompanied Shipment of personal effects		
	International (road)	International staff International staff (families)		
	Local transport (air)	International staff International staff (families) Local staff		

Level 2	Level 3	Level 4,5	Costs =	Foreign	Local
	Local transport (road)	Vehicle type, numbers	*cars* *pick-ups* *4WD* *motorcycles* *other*		
		Purchase or hire Fuel and oil Maintenance and servicing Vehicle insurance, taxes			
Accommod- ation	Travel accommodation	International hotel Local hotel			
	Residential accommoda- tion	Short-term foreign Long-term foreign (single) Long-term foreign (married) Local staff (out-of-office)			
	Office accommodation	Local head office Local site office			
	General	Cost of services and taxes Costs of cleaning and maintenance			

Check list 8. Items covered by the financial proposal

Level 1 — Out-of-pocket expenses (b)

Level 2	Level 3	Level 4,5 Costs =	Foreign	Local
Equipment	Furnishings	Residential Office		
	Computers	Hardware Software		
	Technical	Laboratory equipment Survey equipment		
	General	Local hire or local purchase Permanent transfer Customs and administration		
Insurance tax	Insurance	Staff medical insurance Staff emergency insurance Local company insurance Third party liability insurance Professional liability insurance Employer's liability insurance Equipment insurance Business insurance Property insurance		

Level 2	Level 3	Level 4,5	Costs =	Foreign	Local
	Tax	Company tax Local taxes, duties, fees Income tax Special contributions			
Administra- tion	Telecomm- unications	Standard telephone rental, usage Email, Internet rental, usage Portable telephone rental, usage Other telecommunications			
	Documents	Reproduction, postage			
	Staff	Visas, permits *entry visas* *residence* *work permits* *local medical* *driving licence* Medical certificates Vaccinations			
	Translation	Translation costs Interpreting costs			

Check list 9. Structure and content of the financial proposal

Main section	Typical contents	
Introduction		
Introduction	Title page, edge page	Table of contents
	Submission letter	
Background	Payment schedule	Inflation clauses
notes	Arbitration and mediation	Legal language
	Copy of staffing schedule	Legal jurisdiction
Remuneration		

1. Basic salaries (rates at man–months)	Key personnel
	Backstoppers
		Local key personnel
		Local technical
		  support staff
		Local non-technical
		  support staff

2. Social charges	Leave Financial benefits	Social expenses Miscellaneous
3. Overhead costs	Buildings and equipment Consumables Non-billable staff	Professional expenses Miscellaneous
4. Fee mark-up	Fee mark-up, profit	
Out-of-pocket		
5. Per diem.	Overseas allowance Bonus	Education costs Local staff travel per diem
	Travel per diem Residential per diem	Local staff residential per diem
6. Transport	International transport (air) International transport (road)	Local transport (air) Local transport (road)
7. Accommo-dation	Travel accommodation Residential accommodation	Office accommodation
8. Equipment	Accommodation furnishings Office furnishings	Computer hardware, software
9. Insurance, tax	Staff medical insurance Company insurance Emergency insurance	Company tax Income tax Special contributions*
10. Adminis-tration	Telephone Document reproduction Document postage	E-mail, Internet Staff medical certificates Visas and permits
Summary		
11. Summary tables	Foreign currency(s) Base currency	Local currency
12. Contingencies		
Appendices	Certified company accounts Key staff salary statements	

* Special contributions, such as Germany's reunification tax and some Middle Eastern countries' support for Palestine contributions.
This Check list is copied from Table 37 in chapter 7.

Check list 10. Notes for people working overseas for the first time

General	Detail
International Transport	Check air transport, leave tickets allowance* What is the accompanied luggage allowance? What is the unaccompanied luggage allowance? Is (home-to-airport) transport included?
Accommodation	Will it be acceptable to you/your family?* Is it furnished or unfurnished? Are costs of *all* services included (e.g. telephone)? Will the accommodation be airconditioned? Are meals, cleaning staff etc. provided (for bachelor-status contracts)?
Salary	Are there any local taxes? Do you have to pay home taxes? Does the contract add per diem payments? Does the contract state when and how your salary is to be paid? Does the contract include overtime payments? Will salary be paid for days of travel to/from site?
Medical	Is there free local medical cover? Will you be medically insured (e.g. for further treatment in the UK)?
Local Transport	Is transport provided? Is the site transport available for private use?
Crisis	Does contract include emergency evacuation? Will your salary be paid if you are kidnapped or imprisoned? Will you be the legally responsible representative of the company? Will you be insured against professional error?
Other	Do you have to provide any equipment (e.g. computer)? Does the contract specify what you will have to do? Does the contract specify who you will be responsible to?

* You have different considerations to make, for example
- if you are going to take up a married status or a bachelor appointment
- if you are going on a long-term rather than short-term appointment (say, more than three months).

Check list 11. Contents of project references

Contents	Short	Medium	Long	PR	Lists
Company details	Not needed — covered by other material				
Project details					
Project name	✔	✔	✔	✔	✔
Project reference number	–	–	–	–	✔
Country/location (geographical sector)	✔	✔	✔	✔	✔
Technical sector	✔	✔	✔	✔	✔
Year of completion	✔	✔	✔	✔	✔
Work period (from–to), giving year and month	✔	✔	✔	–	–
Size/length	✔	✔	✔	✔	–
Short description (project, own services)	✔	–	–	✔	–
Expanded description (project, own services)	–	✔	✔	–	–
Full description (project, own services, problems)	–	✔	✔	–	–
Total contract value	–	–	✔	✔	✔
Client details					
Client name	✔	✔	✔	✔	–
Client's project reference number	–	–	–	–	✔
Client address	–	–	✔	–	–
Client contact	–	–	✔	–	–
Your company's input					
Associated firms	–	✔	✔	–	–
Prime consultant or associate firm	–	–	✔	–	–
Man–months input from your company	–	✔	✔	–	–
Man–months input from other companies	–	–	✔	–	–
Value of services provided by your company	✔	✔	✔	✔	✔
Project costs and fees					
Total project cost	✔	✔	✔	✔	–
Consultants fees	–	–	✔	–	✔

Notes

- Make sure that you and your colleagues agree on what each of these items actually means.
- This check list is copied from Table 39 in chapter 12.

Check list 12. Contents of staff references

Contents	Short	Medium	Long	PR	Lists
Personal details					
Name	✔	✔	✔	✔	✔
Nationality	✔	✔	✔	✔	–
Date of birth	✔	✔	✔	–	–
Married status	–	–	–	–	✔
Photograph	–	–	–	✔	–
Profession	✔	✔	✔	✔	✔
Position in present company	✔	✔	✔	✔	–
Years with present company	–	✔	✔	✔	–
Educational qualifications	–	✔	✔	✔	✔
Post-graduation training	–	✔	✔	–	–
Membership of professional bodies	–	✔	✔	–	–
Publications	–	✔	✔	✔	–
Language skills	–	✔	✔	–	✔
Years of professional experience	✔	✔	✔	–	✔
Key qualifications (region, sector experience)	✔	✔	✔	–	–
Project details					
Project name	–	✔	✔	–	–
Country/location (geographical sector)	–	–	✔	✔	–
Technical sector	–	✔	✔	–	–
Year of completion	–	✔	✔	–	–
Work period (from–to)	–	✔	✔	–	–
Size/length	–	✔	✔	–	–
Short description (project, own services)	–	✔	–	–	–
Expanded description (project, own services)	–	–	✔	–	–
Full description (project, own services, problems)	–	–	–	–	–
Client details (= previous employers)					
Client name	✔	✔	✔	–	–
Client address	–	–	–	–	–
Client contact	–	–	–	–	–
Staff member's own input	Not needed — covered by project details				
Project costs and fees					
Total project cost	–	✔	✔	–	–
Consultants fees	–	–	–	–	–

Notes
This Check list is copied from Table 40 in chapter 12.

A1

Definitions

Ad hoc agreements	Association agreement 'for the sole and specific purpose of competing for and undertaking a certain project'.[57]
ADB	Asian Development Bank.
Additional task	Task not specified in the TOR; one that is essential or important to the project.
Advance payments	Payments made on signing a contract for goods or services (e.g. for mobilisation costs) 'usually an advance payment of 10–15% is considered adequate'.[58]
AOTA	Advisory Technical Assistance — the ADB phrase
Applicable law	The law (or laws) governing the contract.
Association chart	A table and diagram which (*a*) lists the partner companies involved in a particular proposal and (*b*) shows the business relationship between them.
Backstopper	An individual from the consultant's home office who is responsible for ensuring the timely provision of backstopping support services.

57 FIDIC *Guide to the use of FIDIC's sub-consultancy and joint venture (consortium) agreements*, page 2, 1994 edition.

58 *World Bank, Disbursement handbook*, 1992, page 45.

Backstopping	Management, technical and administrative support services provided by home office staff.
Bank	A financing institute such as an IFI or a private development bank. Often confused with the client.
Base currency	Currency quoted in the financial proposal which is used to provide common units and totals of the foreign and local cost estimates. The base currency can be either the local currency, one of the foreign currencies, or another, international standard currency such as US dollars.
Beautification	Acceptable improvement of available project references and staff CVs.
Burn out	'A syndrome of physical and emotional exhaustion, involving the development of negative job attitudes and a loss of concern and feeling for those with whom you work'.[59]
Busy	Someone is busy when their working time takes more than half the available calendar time.
Calendar time	Time measured in normal calendar days as opposed to normal company working days.
Client	The person who makes the decisions about the project. He may also be one of the persons who evaluates the proposal. The client may be a representative of a bank but is just as likely to be a government employee in the country where the project is to be built.
Cofinancing	'Project financed by a bank and at least one other external source of funds.'[60]
Consultancy	'Organisation providing advice through general or feasibility studies in various sectors of activity.'[61]

59 *The personal management handbook*, John Mulligan et al, 1992, page 81.

60 *World Bank, Disbursement handbook*, 1992, page 100.

61 Phare registration form for the Phare/Tacis central consultancy register, page 5.

Consultancy firm	Firm which is an independent profit centre with at least two members of full-time professional staff.[62]
Consultant	A partnership, group or association of professional firms — or exceptionally a single self-employed professional person who is part of an established practice or who represents and is backed by such a practice and is accepted by the ODA as an individual independent consultant.[63]
Core team	Key personnel who will be assigned to the project for the full contract period, or for more than six months at a time; long-term personnel, long-term experts.
CVs	Textual descriptions of a person's professional education, training and experience.
DACON	World Bank established system of registering details of consulting companies.
Development division	Regional offices of the UK's ODA.
Discipline	'The primary technological and/or professional capability of individuals in the responding organisation. Possession of an academic degree, professional registration, certification or extensive experience in a particular field of practice normally reflects an individual's primary technical and/or professional discipline.'[64]
EBRD	European Bank for Reconstruction and Development.
EIA	Environmental Impact Assessment.
Engineer	The person in the consulting company bidding for the project, who has to write the proposal.

---

62 Based on the ODA *British overseas aid — arrangements for overseas consultancy services* annex 2, March 1994.

63 ODA's *British overseas aid — arrangements for overseas consultancy* services, page 1, para. 3.

64 UN technical data questionnaire for registration in UN roster (TCD. 176), page 1.

EOI	Expression of Interest.
Executing agency	Government body or department responsible for carrying out a project financed by an ADB (or other bank) loan.
Expatriate personnel	Another phrase for foreign personnel.
Expression of interest (EOI)	The first stage in the formal consultant selection procedure.
Force account	'Civil works executed by a local government agency of the borrower using its own labor force.'[65]
Foreign currency	Currency quoted in the financial proposal which is not the currency of the country the project is to be carried out in (in this sense, what is local currency to you will be foreign currency to the client).
Foreign personnel	Personnel to be employed on the project and who at the time of being hired are resident outside the country the project is situated in.[66] The phrase is also sometimes taken to mean personnel who are not nationals of the client's country — which is not the same thing.
ICB	Internation Competitive Bidding.
IFI	An international financing institution such as the World Bank, the Asian Development Bank or the European Bank for Reconstruction and Development.
International staff	See also foreign personnel.
Joint and several liability	A form of association where (a) the member companies together and (b) each member company individually, can be held financially responsible for the whole of the project.

---

65 *World Bank, Disbursement handbook,* 1992, page 100.

66 *World Bank standard form of contract: consultants services–complex time-based assignments para. 1.1.k.,*
    June 1995

Joint financing	a type of cofinancing 'shared project financing in which funds are independently disbursed from multiple sources in proportion to an agreed ratio'.[67]
Joint venture agreement	'In a joint venture all parties to the Agreement will have considerable influence on the working decisions of the team and will almost always carry joint and several liability. Many clients see this as a major advantage of a joint venture.'[68]
Key personnel	The specialists who are to be employed on the project (phrases also used include key staff); the key personnel can include both international and local staff.
Key themes	The main selling points of your technical proposal.
Language	The language which is 'the binding and controlling language for all matters relating to the meaning or interpretation of the contract';[69] there should be only one language for the project.
Lead company	The member company of a joint venture association which is authorised to represent the joint venture in matters concerning the project contract and the execution of the works. (Other phrases include member in charge).
Local currency	Currency quoted in the financial proposal which is the currency of the country in which the project is to be carried out.
Local knowledge	Familiarity with the technical and non-technical background of the region or country in which a project is to be carried out; the difference between a good and a mediocre proposal.

---

67 *World Bank, Disbursement handbook*, 1992, page 100.

68 FIDIC's *Guide to the use of FIDIC's sub-consultancy and joint venture (consortium) agreements*, page 3, 1994 edition.

69 *World Bank standard form of contract: consultants services–complex time-based assignments* para. 1.4., June, 1995

Local personnel	Personnel to be employed on the project and who at the time of being hired are resident in the country the project is situated in.[70] The phrase is also sometimes taken to mean personnel who are nationals of the client's country — which is not the same thing.
Long-term personnel	'Foreign personnel staying for twelve or more consecutive months in the (project) country',[71] usually, members of the core team; also usually long-term experts.
Lump sum contracts	Consultancy contracts based on a fixed lump sum for the full services as defined in the contract.
Optional task	Task not specified in the TOR; one that is not essential to the project, but which the client might like as an extra service (and which the client would expect extra fees for).
Parallel financing	A type of cofinancing 'shared project financing in which selected goods or services are financed separately by the bank and each of the other financial sources'.[72]
Per diem allowance	Daily personal allowance paid to staff working away from their home office, and used to cover incidental costs incurred such as food and local transport.
Permanent staff	Staff who are and have been full-time employees of the company for more than twelve consecutive months.
PPF	Project Preparation Facility 'advance commitment to a borrower by the Bank to provide financial and technical assistance to prepare a new project, prior to approval of the final loan'.[73]

70 *World Bank standard form of contract: consultants services–complex time-based assignments* para. 1.1.k., June, 1995

71 *World Bank standard form of contract: consultants services–complex time-based assignments* para. 6.3.(b)(viii). June, 199572 *World Bank, Disbursement handbook*, 1992, page 101.

72 *World Bank, Disbursement handbook*, 1992, page 101.

73 *World Bank, Disbursement handbook*, 1992, page 101.

PPTA	Project Preparation Technical Assistance — the ADB phrase for technical assistance projects.
PQ	Pre-qualification document; the second stage in the formal consultant selection procedure.
Pressure	A measure of the stress someone is working under.
Price adjustment clauses	Clauses in a contract where prices may be subject to upward or downward movement, for example due to exchange rate fluctuations or increase in staff costs (salaries).
Project pipeline	A general term for the various procedures and stages which schemes pass through while a bank is considering providing finance for them.
Proposal	A costed offer to carry out a specified consultancy service.
Proposed projects	Schemes which a bank is *considering* providing finance for.
REG	Regional Technical Assistance — an ADB phrase.
Relevant pressure	An indication of the stress someone is working under and which is due to their involvement in your project or proposal.
Short-term experts	Key personnel who will be assigned to the project for less than the full contract period, and for maximum three to six months at a time 'personnel with less than twelve months consecutive stay in the (project) country'.[74]
SME	'Small and medium enterprises: those firms (whether or not a subsidiary of larger concerns) having less than 200 employees.'[75]

---

74 *World Bank standard form of contract: consultants services–complex time-based assignments* para. 6.3(b)(iii) June 1995.

75 ODA *index of consulting firms, registration application amendment* (February 1996).

Staff, full-time	Permanent, professional staff employed full-time, including staff of affiliates with which you operate as an entity.'[76]
Staff, part-time professional	'Part-time staff under standing contractual arrangements who are regularly employed as experts for special missions and are permanently available for future assignments.'[76]
Sub-consultancy agreement	An alternative to a joint venture agreement, 'where one of the consultants has only a small, well-defined input'.[77]
Target country	The country in which the project (for which the proposal is being prepared) is to be carried out.
Task	The main steps in the process you would follow to carry out the services required by the new project.
Teamwork management	As in *those who can, do — those who manage, help them do it.*
Technical cooperation	May include projects such as pre-feasibility and feasibility studies, and advice on management and operation, but not on detailed designs, preparation of tender or contract documents, or construction supervision.
Time-based contracts	Consultancy contracts based on the staff time actually used to carry out the contract.
TOR	Terms of Reference: the documents which accompany an invitation to submit a proposal for a project, and which give some background information about the work involved and the client's special requirements.
TOR task	Task specified in the TOR.

---

76 World Bank, *DACON registration guide*, page 23, 1994.

77 FIDIC, *Guide to the use of FIDIC's sub-consultancy and joint venture (consortium) agreements*, page 3, 1994 edition.

Travel time	Time for foreign personnel to travel from their home office to the project site; usually included in the period of assignment of the foreign personnel.
Two-envelope system	A system in which the technical and financial proposals are submitted in two separate, sealed envelopes, and in which

- in theory, the financial proposals are only opened when the technical proposals have been evaluated, but
- in practice, the financial proposals are opened first and the most expensive submissions are immediately rejected.

Working time	That period of calendar time during when someone is fully occupied with meaningful work.

A2

Suggested reading

The following is simply a *starter list* of publications which you should consider reading. In general, try to read anything you can find on the target country together with anything you can get your hands on about the financing institutions including their Internet home pages.

Asian Development Bank (1993). *ADB guidelines for incorporation of social dimensions in bank operations*. Oct.

Asian Development Bank (1996). *ADB basic information*. Jan.

Asian Development Bank (1996). *Guidelines on the use of consultants by the ADB and its borrowers*. Reprint.*

DACON (Data on consultants) consulting firm registration form (Form 1600 (11/88)) as issued by financing institutions such as the Asian Development Bank. Also available are *Guide to completing the DACON form financial services sector — supplement to the Dacon registration form* and *Guide to completing the supplement to the DACON registration form*.

The Economist (1996). *The Economist style guide*. Profile Publishing.

The Economist Intelligence Unit Country forecasts.

European Bank for Reconstruction and Development (1993). *EBRD information for consultants*. Mar.*

European Bank for Reconstruction and Development (1993). *EBRD guide to procurement opportunities*.*

European Bank for Reconstruction and Development (1995). *Annual Report 1994*.

European Bank for Reconstruction and Development (1996). *Annual Report 1995*.

European Bank for Reconstruction and Development (1996). Information sheets (various subjects).

European Bank for Reconstruction and Development (1996). *EBRD directory of business information sources*.

European Bank for Reconstruction and Development (1996). *Guide to publications.* Mar.

European Bank for Reconstruction and Development (1996). *EBRD procurement policies and rules.* Rev. Mar.

European Bank for Reconstruction and Development (1996). *Financing with the EBRD.* Rev. Mar.

European Investment Bank (1995). *Annual Report 1994.*

European Investment Bank (1995 edn). *Die Europäische Investitionsbank — Finanzierungsinstituion der Europäische Union.*

European Investment Bank (1996). *EIB information, No. 87.* Feb.

FIDIC (International Federation of Consulting Engineers) (1980). *FIDIC guidelines and terms of reference for the preparation of project cost estimates.*

FIDIC (1991). *Selection by ability — guidelines on quality-based selection of consulting engineers.**

FIDIC (1992). *Program management by the consulting engineer.*

FIDIC (1994 edn). *Guide to the use of FIDIC's sub-consultancy and joint venture (consortium) agreements.**

FIDIC (1994) *Tendering procedure — procedure for obtaining and evaluating tenders for civil engineering contracts.**

FIDIC (1995). *Improving transfer of technology — guide to actions.*

FIDIC (1997). *Quality-based selection for the procurement of consulting services.*

Hammer M. and Champy J. (1994). *Re-engineering the corporation.* Harperbusiness.*

Hopkins T. (1988). *How to master the art of selling.* Grafton Books.*

Litke H-D. (1991). *Projektmanagement — Methoden, Techniken,*

Verhaltensweisen. Carl Hanser Verlag, Munich.*

Moody-Stuart G. (1996). *Grand corruption.* Worldview Publications.

OPEC fund for international development (1982). *Procurement guidelines under loans extended by the OPEC fund.* Nov.

OPEC fund for international development (1983). *Disbursement procedures.* May.

OPEC fund for international development (1995). *OPEC annual report 1994.*

OPEC fund for international development (1995). OPEC fund newsletters for 1995. Published every four months.

Overseas Development Administration (1994). *British overseas aid — arrangements for overseas consultancy services.* RE 150, Mar.*

Overseas Development Administration (1994). *Index of consulting firms — registration application.* Sept.*

Overseas Development Administration (1995). *ODA know-how-fund annual report.*

Tutt P. and Adler D. eds. (1990). *New metric handbook; planning and design data.* Butterworth Architecture.*

United Nations Development Programme (1996). *United Nations system — general business guide.* July, 16th edn. Inter-Agency Procurement Services Office.*

World Bank (1992). *Disbursement handbook.* July.*

World Bank (1995). *DACON registration guide.**

World Bank (1995). *World Bank standard form of contract: consultants services — complex time-based assignments.* June.*

World Bank (1995). *World Bank standard form of contract, consultants services — lump sum remuneration.* June.

World Bank (1995). *Guidelines for use of consultants by World Bank borrowers and the World Bank as executing agency.* July, reprint.

World Bank (1995). *The World Bank Group — Directory.* Nov.

World Bank (1995). *The World Bank Group — Guide to international business opportunities in projects funded by the World Bank.* 3rd edn, Dec.*

World Bank (1996). *Index of publications and guide to information products and services.* Jan.

World Bank (1996). *Guidelines for procurement under IBRD (International Bank for Reconstruction and Development) loans and IDA (International Development Association) credits.* Aug.

* Referred to in footnotes.